The trial of Count Struensee, late Prime Minister to the King of Denmark, before the Royal Commission of Inquisition, at Copenhagen. Translated from the Danish and German originals.

Johann Friedrich Struensee

ECCO
PRINT EDITIONS

The trial of Count Struensee, late Prime Minister to the King of Denmark, before the Royal Commission of Inquisition, at Copenhagen. Translated from the Danish and German originals.

Struensee, Johann Friedrich, greve
ESTCID: T100341
Reproduction from British Library
Contains: 'The memorial of accusation in behalf of the Crown, against Count John Fred. Struensee', 'The memorial of defence in behalf of Count John Fred. Struensee','The defence of Count John Fred. Struensee',written by himself', 'The judgement of the Roy
London : printed for the translator; sold by T. Waters; T. Axtell; and J. Whitaker, 1775.
viii,76,[2],78-79,81-150p. ; 8°

Eighteenth Century
Collections Online
Print Editions

Gale ECCO Print Editions

Relive history with *Eighteenth Century Collections Online*, now available in print for the independent historian and collector. This series includes the most significant English-language and foreign-language works printed in Great Britain during the eighteenth century, and is organized in seven different subject areas including literature and language; medicine, science, and technology; and religion and philosophy. The collection also includes thousands of important works from the Americas.

The eighteenth century has been called "The Age of Enlightenment." It was a period of rapid advance in print culture and publishing, in world exploration, and in the rapid growth of science and technology – all of which had a profound impact on the political and cultural landscape. At the end of the century the American Revolution, French Revolution and Industrial Revolution, perhaps three of the most significant events in modern history, set in motion developments that eventually dominated world political, economic, and social life.

In a groundbreaking effort, Gale initiated a revolution of its own: digitization of epic proportions to preserve these invaluable works in the largest online archive of its kind. Contributions from major world libraries constitute over 175,000 original printed works. Scanned images of the actual pages, rather than transcriptions, recreate the works *as they first appeared.*

Now for the first time, these high-quality digital scans of original works are available via print-on-demand, making them readily accessible to libraries, students, independent scholars, and readers of all ages.

For our initial release we have created seven robust collections to form one the world's most comprehensive catalogs of 18th century works.

Initial Gale ECCO Print Editions collections include:

History and Geography
Rich in titles on English life and social history, this collection spans the world as it was known to eighteenth-century historians and explorers. Titles include a wealth of travel accounts and diaries, histories of nations from throughout the world, and maps and charts of a world that was still being discovered. Students of the War of American Independence will find fascinating accounts from the British side of conflict.

Social Science

Delve into what it was like to live during the eighteenth century by reading the first-hand accounts of everyday people, including city dwellers and farmers, businessmen and bankers, artisans and merchants, artists and their patrons, politicians and their constituents. Original texts make the American, French, and Industrial revolutions vividly contemporary.

Medicine, Science and Technology

Medical theory and practice of the 1700s developed rapidly, as is evidenced by the extensive collection, which includes descriptions of diseases, their conditions, and treatments. Books on science and technology, agriculture, military technology, natural philosophy, even cookbooks, are all contained here.

Literature and Language

Western literary study flows out of eighteenth-century works by Alexander Pope, Daniel Defoe, Henry Fielding, Frances Burney, Denis Diderot, Johann Gottfried Herder, Johann Wolfgang von Goethe, and others. Experience the birth of the modern novel, or compare the development of language using dictionaries and grammar discourses.

Religion and Philosophy

The Age of Enlightenment profoundly enriched religious and philosophical understanding and continues to influence present-day thinking. Works collected here include masterpieces by David Hume, Immanuel Kant, and Jean-Jacques Rousseau, as well as religious sermons and moral debates on the issues of the day, such as the slave trade. The Age of Reason saw conflict between Protestantism and Catholicism transformed into one between faith and logic -- a debate that continues in the twenty-first century.

Law and Reference

This collection reveals the history of English common law and Empire law in a vastly changing world of British expansion. Dominating the legal field is the *Commentaries of the Law of England* by Sir William Blackstone, which first appeared in 1765. Reference works such as almanacs and catalogues continue to educate us by revealing the day-to-day workings of society.

Fine Arts

The eighteenth-century fascination with Greek and Roman antiquity followed the systematic excavation of the ruins at Pompeii and Herculaneum in southern Italy; and after 1750 a neoclassical style dominated all artistic fields. The titles here trace developments in mostly English-language works on painting, sculpture, architecture, music, theater, and other disciplines. Instructional works on musical instruments, catalogs of art objects, comic operas, and more are also included.

The BiblioLife Network

This project was made possible in part by the BiblioLife Network (BLN), a project aimed at addressing some of the huge challenges facing book preservationists around the world. The BLN includes libraries, library networks, archives, subject matter experts, online communities and library service providers. We believe every book ever published should be available as a high-quality print reproduction; printed on-demand anywhere in the world. This insures the ongoing accessibility of the content and helps generate sustainable revenue for the libraries and organizations that work to preserve these important materials.

The following book is in the "public domain" and represents an authentic reproduction of the text as printed by the original publisher. While we have attempted to accurately maintain the integrity of the original work, there are sometimes problems with the original work or the micro-film from which the books were digitized. This can result in minor errors in reproduction. Possible imperfections include missing and blurred pages, poor pictures, markings and other reproduction issues beyond our control. Because this work is culturally important, we have made it available as part of our commitment to protecting, preserving, and promoting the world's literature.

GUIDE TO FOLD-OUTS MAPS and OVERSIZED IMAGES

The book you are reading was digitized from microfilm captured over the past thirty to forty years. Years after the creation of the original microfilm, the book was converted to digital files and made available in an online database.

In an online database, page images do not need to conform to the size restrictions found in a printed book. When converting these images back into a printed bound book, the page sizes are standardized in ways that maintain the detail of the original. For large images, such as fold-out maps, the original page image is split into two or more pages

Guidelines used to determine how to split the page image follows:

• Some images are split vertically; large images require vertical and horizontal splits.
• For horizontal splits, the content is split left to right.
• For vertical splits, the content is split from top to bottom.
• For both vertical and horizontal splits, the image is processed from top left to bottom right.

THE

TRIAL

OF

COUNT

JOHN FRED. STRUENSEE,

Late PRIME MINISTER of DENMARK.

[Price Two-Shillings and Six-Pence, fewed.]

THE
TRIAL
OF
COUNT STRUENSEE,

LATE PRIME MINISTER

TO

THE KING OF DENMARK,

BEFORE THE

ROYAL COMMISSION

OF

INQUISITION,

AT COPENHAGEN.

Tranflated from the DANISH and GERMAN Originals.

LONDON,

PRINTED FOR THE TRANSLATOR;

Sold by T. WATERS, South-Audley-Street, Grofvenor-
Square, T. AXTELL, under the Royal-Exchange, and
J. WHITAKER, in Mitre-Court, Fleet-Street.
M DCC LXXV.

THE

TRANSLATOR's

PREFACE.

THE late Revolution in Denmark, which has so much attracted the attention of all Europe, has been more particularly interesting to England than to any other Nation. The source of this event has hitherto been clouded with obscurity; but Time, that certain unraveller of all secrets, has now dispelled the mist, and laid the prospect open to our view. The English Reader is here at last presented with the Trial of Count *Struensee*, wherein not only *his* crimes, but also *many other* interesting circumstances, which occasioned that scene of horror and confusion, are set in their proper light, by the most eminent Danish Judges and Counsellors.

It may perhaps be thought necessary, that, for certain reasons, some apology should be made for the publication of the following sheets, though they indisputably clear up a *doubt* that has been long fluttering in the bofoms of many Englifhmen; and it may probably be alledged, that the errors of thofe, who have taken a long farewel to the momentary buftle of this life, fhould be for ever buried in oblivion.

It is, indeed, as *ufelefs* as *cruel* to arraign the paft errors and follies of private individuals, who, when they ftep afide from the paths of honour and virtue, bring the evil effects of it on themfelves, without fenfibly injuring the ftate; but it is not fo with thofe who are either born or raifed to exalted ftations, and to whom we look up for examples of honour, probity and virtue. The facred page of Hiftory, which muft not be influenced by any partial confideration, will reprefent their characters in their genuine light, either as deferving the imitation of Sovereigns yet unborn, or hold them up on high as beacons, to caution the heedlefs royal mariners againft thofe dangerous rocks, which lie hidden in the tremendous bofom of the deep. We, therefore, as a Plea for this publication, beg leave to quote that fublime fentence of Lord Mansfield :——— *Fiat juftitia, ruat cœlum* !

It is not the wifh of the Tranflator of this work to draw a veil over an illuftrious family, an offspring of which is fo materially concerned therein ;—the loftieft and moft ftately oak may, by furious and unrelenting blafts, be deprived of one of its fineft branches, and yet remain the Pride and Glory of the foreft. Whatever may have been the weaknefles of the late and truly-unfortunate Queen of Denmark, yet the following pages will incontrovertibly prove, even upon

the

the authority of his Danish Majesty's best friends and most humble dependants, that her crime, however unpardonable in the eyes of *rigid* Virtue, abounds with many alleviating circumstances.

Bred amidst the false glare, luxury and hypocrisy, of a court; transplanted in the bloom of her youth, from under the care of a tender mother, into a distant climate, and slighted to all appearance by him in whom all her future hopes of happiness centered;—is it a wonder that Passion and Prejudice should prevail over Reason and Prudence?

The unfortunate victim to unbounded Ambition, who is now *deservedly* no more, would never have presumed (it is more than reasonable to suppose) to corrupt royal innocence and virtue, had not *royal folly* in her consort made the *secret* assistance and skill of a person of his profession absolutely necessary. From hence arose that fatal intimacy, which a daring and ambitious individual improved to his ruin.

With regard to the authenticity of this Work, the Translator thinks it needless to say any thing, since that will evidently appear to every Reader who shall peruse it. Every possible care has been taken, that the translation should faithfully convey the true meaning of the original papers from which it is taken; and for this purpose several persons in Copenhagen have been consulted, in order to clear up some particulars which appeared obscure.

In the Defence of *Struenfee* will be found many fin-
gular Anecdotes of the Danifh Court, which not only
elucidate many circumftances of this melancholy tranfaction, but alfo explore the intrigues and cabals of
courtiers, and may likewife prove ferviceable to the
writer, who fhall hereaftei attempt the Hiftory of Denmark at this period.   The Plea of the Attorney-General in behalf of the Crown, the Reply of *Struenfee*'s
Counfel thereto, and the Judgement of the Royal
Court of Inquifition, are crowded with many interefi-
ing circumftances ; but, that we may not appear partial by giving our opinion thereon, we fhall here pafs
them over in filence, and leave them to be noticed,
canvaffed, and applauded or condemned, when the
judicious Reader fhall meet with them in the following pages.   **12 JY 62**

THE

MEMORIAL of ACCUSATION

IN

BEHALF OF THE CROWN,

AGAINST

COUNT JOHN FRED. STRUENSEE,

Late Prime Minister of Denmark, &c,

LAID BEFORE THE

ROYAL COMMISSION of INQUISITION,

At COPENHAGEN, April 20, 1772.

By His Danish Majesty's Attorney General.

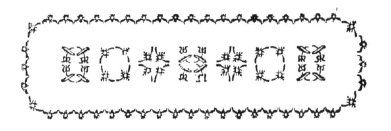

Memorial of Accufation, &c.

MY LORDS,

ON the 10th inft. I laid before this moft honourable court, his Majefty's moft gracious commands, to plead in behalf of the crown againft the two Counts, *John Frederick Strvenfee*, and *Enewold Brandt*, and to accufe them feparately of their refpective crimes. On the fame day I proceeded on this action, according to the forms prefcribed by law, and I now lay before this honourable court this Memorial of Accufation againft Count *John Frederick Strvenfee*, with the neceffary deductions, and the proofs of his different crimes.

It is a maxim founded on truth, that a fevere and ftrict government can never be of long duration, and that tyrannical and oppreffive rulers may be productive of more mifchief in one year, than the wifdom of whole ages can amend. The inhabitants of Denmark and Norway have, for many centuries, been ufed to a mild and lenient

government.

government. Their love and affection for their sovereign have ever been unimpeachable, and have always intitled them to royal and paternal affection, which they have enjoyed uninterrupted through a series of reigns. They are, in general, a virtuous and quiet people; they have a due reverence for the Almighty Being, and worship him in sincerity of heart. Our country has long been the seat of domestic harmony and happiness: every subject has here lived secure, and strangers have sought this soil as the asylum of safety and security. But, within these few years, every thing has worn a very different aspect. The King has been rendered obnoxious in the eyes of the people, and the people have been represented to his Majesty as unworthy their Sovereign's affection. No one could approach the King, but those who belonged to the junto of those miscreants, who, under the specious pretence of being the KING's FRIENDS (*), were his greatest enemies. Insolence, audacity, and infamy, dared to approach the throne, and stamped the immaculate lustre of the royal house with indelible reproach. Every thing sacred and religious was turned into ridicule and mockery; virtue and decency were banished, and shame and infamy, with their innumerable train of vices, usurped their sacred seat, and to these angels of darkness the people were taught to look up as to examples

(*) The English probably borrowed from the Danes their modern phrase of THE KING's FRIENDS, since in Denmark, as well as in England, it seems to convey to our idea a set of men, who flatter to betray, who sacrifice their country to self-interested views, and who, like the serpent, press the earth with their bellies, only that they may spring forward

examples worthy of imitation. Indeed, audacity went even so far, that the highest sovereign power, with which the subjects had chearfully invested King Frederick III. and his successors, was now to be executed by a mean and unworthy subject, and a plan was laid for its extension, in order that the miscreant, who assumed the royal authority, might rule with unlimitted sway, and in greater security. The nation and the language of the country were both despised alike. Every thing was to be modelled according to the fancy of a german favourite. Persons in places and offices, who had long served their King and country faithfully, were dismissed, and strangers, or worthless sycophants, substituted in their places. I leave it to every friend of his country to judge what effects these innovations, and a court formed on such principles, could possibly produce. Every true born Dane shuddered with horror to see his country plunged into ruin and destruction. Sorrow and grief were painted on the face of the whole nation, and their sentiments of disapprobation to the new-fangled mode of government, were sufficiently expressed by anonymous publications, in which an oppressed and enslaved people breathed forth such complaints, as are ever terrible and alarming to the ears of despotic ministers, who well know and dread, that a cloud in the political hemisphere threatens an approaching storm. In short, our country was no more the land of domestic harmony and happiness. The destruction of whole families was no longer considered as an injury to society; in a word, Denmark wore the appearance of Egypt, at the time when the destroying Angel had performed his circuit. —But who was our destroying Angel?

B 3

I hear

I hear the whole nation confirm my anfwer, it was *John Frederick Struenfee*, the moft daring and ambitious mortal that ever figured on the furface of the terraqueous globe; and who, in this re-fpect, may be called, " *Vir unius feculi.*" He was formerly a phyfician, and is now a count; but before I leave him, he fhall have nothing left of his grandeur but horror, fentence, and that pu-nifhment, which juftice and the whole nation cries aloud for at your hands.

John Frederick Struenfee was born at Halle, in the year 1737. He there ftudied phyfic, and took his degrees. In the year 1758, by friends and intereft, he obtained the place of phyfician in ordinary to the city of Altona, where (according to the proverb) he foon affumed the character of " *Medicus veniam accidendi per totam urbem,*" which prerogative he alfo endeavoured to affume after-wards as prime-minifter, *per utrumque regnum.*

Impudence and ignorance are infeparable com-panions; and thefe, or an uncommon fhare of abili-ties, muft have induced him to accept, at the age of twenty-one, the important truft of phyfician in ordinary to the city of Altona—a truft, which had ever been cautioufly granted to fuch only, whofe age and experience placed them at the head of their profeffion. It is moft probable, that im-pudence, rather than merit, raifed him to this employ, fince, if we may judge of his *medical* by his *political* knowledge, we fhall be compelled to conclude, that the poifonous medicines he admi-niftered, as phyfician, were as fatal at Altona, as were the political draughts, which, as a ftatefman, he forced down the throats of the Danes. It may indeed be alledged, that, if at Altona he increafed the number of the dead, the effects of his gal-

lanties

lantries and intrigues in some measure made up for the loss (*). Rumour flies swiftly, and, like the shadow, keeps close to the object that causes it. I speak nothing merely from my own knowledge, but from the different acts and records before this honourable commission. In these, amongst others, I find Count *Enevold Branat*'s declaration: that it has been well known of *Struensee*, that seven or eight years have passed since he began to treat religion with contempt, that he was fond of women, with whom he always took great liberties, and into whose favour he never failed to insinuate himself.

After having spent nearly ten years as physician at Altona, he became acquainted with Count *Brandt*, to whom he expressed his desire to obtain a place at court. Count *Brandt* accordingly employed his good offices in *Struensee*'s behalf, at the time when his Majesty proposed to make a tour into foreign countries, and, as a physician was

not

(*) The Danish counsellor appears here to have taken a step too far. He attributes *Struensee*'s success at Altona, either to *impudence* or *an uncommon share of abilities*. He has by no means cleared up this point, but absolutely attributes that to *impudence*, which the candid and disinterested reader may perhaps place to the account of *merit*. That a man shall be an *ignorant* physician, merely because he is a *bad* statesman, is a conclusion none but a lawyer will presume to draw The long time this unfortunate man figured in the world, surely afforded sufficient opportunity for getting at the truth of this matter, which might have been so easily obtained. The medical abilities of *Struensee* do not appear to have suffered in his treatment of the King, on *more* occasions than *one*, in the course of his travels with that monarch; and, if we may credit some anecdotes of the Danish court, lately published, her Majesty herself was under some private obligations to the medical skill of the Count, and which seems to have laid the foundation for more intimate connections.

not thought superfluous in the retinue of a Monarch, *Struensee* met with the accomplishment of his wishes, and in the year 1768, was appointed physician in ordinary to his Majesty, during his travels. I have authentic accounts, that during the whole journey, he led a loose and profligate life. God and religion were the constant objects of his mockery. Every one, who had the honour of attending his Majesty in his tour, will testify the truth of what I have here advanced for two reasons: first, because in criminal matters, we ought to omit nothing that promises to explore to our view the actions and character of the criminal; and secondly, to invalidate Count *Struensee*'s hypocritical excuses, that he had never made religion the object of his ridicule.

Count *Struensee*, long before his appointment at court, had been pregnant with the idea of making his fortune at the expence of the Danish and Norwegian nation, and that at any rate whatever. The frequent opportunity of being about the King's person, during his travels, contributed greatly to hasten the execution of his plan; and he failed not to draw from it every advantage that art and cunning could obtain. He studied the passions and inclinations of the King, and through that channel found an easy passage to his heart. He became his favourite.

When his Majesty returned from his travels, *Struensee* appeared at court in the capacity only of a physician, but as the state counsellers, *Berger* and *Piper*, men grown old and experienced in their profession, were then physicians in ordinary to the King, there was no room for this criminal to advance through that channel. This, however, proved no check to his ambition; for he

was

was soon appointed reader to the King. His art, cunning, and hypocrify, had then a copious field to revel on ; and he so effectually employed this favourable opportunity, that he soon rivetted himself in the favour and confidence of the King.

Moderation should have taught him to be satisfied with a situation infinitely above his extraction and abilities ; but ambition, like the troubled billows of the boundless ocean, is never to be confined · It is the punishment of ambitious souls, never to be satisfied ; and an insatiable thirst for power and grandeur, when it once takes root in the human bosom, never quits its unhappy possessor till it plunges him into the abyss of disgrace and ruin. *Struenfee*, like Cæsar, could not brook the thoughts of an equal : He determined to be absolute master over every one that surrounded him, and resolved to be the first man in the kingdom, if not in name and person, in power and authority at least.

I shall proceed regularly through the different means he employed to obtain the gratification of his wishes, in the same order as I find them stated by his own declaration, by that of the different witnesses who were examined, and by many other circumstances in the records before this Honourable Commiffion.

The first step he took towards the summit of his ambition, is an act so daring and audacious, that horror and indignation seizes every honest mind at the very idea thereof, and plainly shews, that no crimes, even those of the blackest dye, were able to deter him from the vain pursuit of power and glory, at the expence of virtue, by the seduction of innocence, and by wresting from his royal master the dearest object of his felicity

(of

(of this I fhall fay more hereafter.) Having, however, fucceeded in this, he began to
fhew himfelf, at a diftance, the man he intended
to be. But he found it foon inconvenient to ferve
two mafters at once. He feared that his Hypocrify and treachery might foon or late be difcovered. Being a ftranger in the country, and having no powerful connections to fupport him in
the purfuit of his mighty plan, he confidered precaution, or more properly fpeaking hypocrify and
deceit, as in fome meafure neceffary. He redou-
bled his affiduity in attending the perfon of the
King, which he confidered as the more indifpenfi-
ble, fince he thereby fruftrated every attempt that
might be made, by any honeft individual, to open
the King's eyes to a fenfe of his miftake, and to
the ruin of *Struenfee*. But this affiduity hindered
him in many refpects from the gratification of his
wifhes, and from thofe actions, which it was neceffary to hide from his Majefty. He therefore
thought that a trufty friend, in whom he could
confide, might be of infinite fervice to him in
the Execution of his plan. His views were directed on *Enewold Brandt*, who fome time before,
had incurred his Majefty's difpleafure, and had
been forbidden the court. He certainly could not
have fingled out a fitter fubject and better companion to his iniquitous projects, than this *Brandt*,
whom he knew thoroughly, and was perfuaded
that his pliant foul was to be moulded into any
form in which he fhould wifh to fee it. He confidered farther, that by reftoring *Brandt* to the
King's favours, he fhould lay a lafting obligation
on the Man, of whom he meant to make a tool,
and that, by the great advantages, riches, and
honours, he propofed to procure him, he hoped
firmly

firmly to attach him to his intereſt. On this ground he proceeded; the way before him was open, and he reached the goal with little difficulty. For the proof of all this, I refer this Honourable Court to his original pompous letter to his friend in iniquity, which is upon the records, and in which he expreſſes himſelf thus: "*Après avoir* "*gagné la confiance du Roi, les faveurs de la Reine,* "*& le credit dans le public, & cela par mes propres* "*forces, avec tout le riſque & toutes les peines at-* "*tachées à une telle entrepriſe, que vous n'auriez cer-* "*tainement pas ſupporté, & laquelle, j'oſe l'aſſurer,* "*vous n'auriez certainement pas pu finir, je vous* "*appelle, & je partage avec vous tout l'effet, & tous* "*les agrémens, qui en peuvent reſulter.*" (*) Count *Brandt* accordingly appeared again at court, and ſoon after obtained Count *Warnſtedt*'s place, as conſtant companion to his Majeſty. His princi-pal buſineſs was, (according to his inſtructions from *Struenſee*) to obſerve the King cloſely, to take all the care poſſible, that none but friends to their party ſhould find admiſſion to his Majeſty, and whenever that happened, to obſerve what was ſaid, and in what diſpoſition the King might ap-pear. All theſe commiſſions Count *Brandt* executed very ſtrictly, and the advantages *Struenſee* reaped from his ſervices are clearly to be ſeen in his an-ſwer

---

(*) To aſſiſt the Engliſh reader, who may not be acquainted with the French language, we ſhall tranſlate this and the fol-lowing paſſages quoted from the original papers — " After " having gained the confidence of the King, the *favours* " of the Queen, and credit among the public, and theſe " by my own addreſs, in ſpite of all the toils and dangers " annexed to ſuch an attempt, (which you certainly would " never have been able to ſupport, and leſs likely to accom-" pliſh) I call you to partake with me all the honours and " advantages that may reſult from my labours."

fwer to Count *Brandt*'s admonifhing letter, in which the latter expreffed his doubts, that all thefe machinations would not be of long duration, that the whole would have a bad end, and therefore intimated a defire to withdraw himfelf in time. *Struenfee* encouraged him to remain in his place, in the following Words: " *Examinez votre pofition* " *& les motifs qui vous y tiennent, rangez d un coté* " *les agrémens, & de l'autre les défagrémens, &* " *comparez cela avec vos fituations paffées, & avec* " *ceux auquels vous vous pouvez attendre, & faites* " *alors la conclufion.*" (*) All what I have here faid appears upon the records before this Honourable Court, and is according to Count *Brandt*'s own declaration, during his examination on the 2d of March.

Count *Struenfee*, finding himfelf thus provided with a trufty friend, to watch the motions of the King, now purfued his plan in greater fecurity, and began to act as mafter. He increafed the number of adherents to his party, by introducing men deftitute of capacity for the management of ftate matters, and who were incapable of doing the leaft fervice to their country; but, like him, felf-intereft was their fole purfuit.

The firft obftacle to the abfolute government of this daring man was his Majefty's moft Honourable Privy Council, which confifted of men of the higheft rank and firft abilities in the kingdom;

(*) " Reflect on your fituation, and the motives which there " retain you. Place on one fide the pleafures you enjoy, " and on the other the toils you endure. Compare thefe " with your late fituation, and what now lies in full profpect " before you From hence draw your conclufion."

kingdom, who were thoroughly acquainted with the laws and conftitution of this country, and who had been trained up, from their youth, to the ftudy of politics. This council was accordingly diffolved and difmiffed, under the fpecious pretence, that his Majefty finding himfelf conftrained from ufing his abfolute royal authority, intended to difpatch all bufinefs with greater expedition from his own cabinet. But the motive of this, and many other proceedings, was foon perceived. It was not to extend his Majefty's prerogative, which had never been conftrained by his Privy Council, but to extend *Struenfee*'s power and authority, who foon after affumed the character of Prime Minifter, and appeared as the Man, to whom both Nations, of what rank and character foever, were to pay due obedience, and whofe commands, figned by himfelf, had the fame force and authority as thofe figned by the King. Thus, this ambitious man, ignorant of the language, laws and conftitution, the political and commercial intereft of the country, undertook to execute the bufinefs of the two kingdoms, which before him had given full employment to fo many able and experienced ftatefmen.

While he was flattering himfelf with the power he had ufurped, the difcerning part of the Nation with pleafure beheld him raifed to that precipice of ftate, from which he muft foon fall into the ocean of ruin and oblivion, and thereby fave the Kingdom from total deftruction. This Prime Minifter was conftantly furrounded by fchemers and projectors, who, like himfelf, underftood nothing of what they were about. Every thing was new modelled, and upon principles the moft deftructive, for whatever the ignorance of the

Minifter

Minifter fuggefted, the applaufes of his fervile de-
pendents confirmed. Integrity and virtue afforded
no fecurity to the poffeffors of places, who were difmiffed at a moment's notice, to make room for fome
defperate creature of his own party. Thus men of
diftinguifhed abilities, to whom their country owed
much, were deprived of the means of fubfiftance,
and their families expofed to famine, mifery, and
defpair. As a proof of this, and the impudence
wherewith he purfued his fecret views, I fhall only
mention the appointment of his own brother. This
man was a profeffor of mathematicks at *Lignitz,*
in *Silefia,* and him he propofed as the fitteft perfon
to fuperintend his Majefty's finances in both kingdoms of Denmark and Norway. This man might
probably have been a very good mathematician;
(though our country was not deftitute of very able
men in that fcience) but of the finances in Denmark and Norway he certainly knew as much, as
a blind man knows of aftronomy. His appointment,
therefore, to that place had no other motive with
the Minifter, than to fecure to himfelf the royal
treafure, into which he has made many confiderable grafps, both for himfelf and his trufty friends.
Many thoufands were frequently embezzled, and
even fums of 60,000 dollars were taken, in a fraudulent manner, from his Majefty's treafury, without his knowledge and confent. Of this alfo I
fhall fay more hereafter

Having thus acquired the higheft power, yet in
appearance under fome reftrictions, he has in every
refpect exceeded its boundaries. It was his Majefty's pleafure, that all orders from the cabinet,
which he himfelf had not verbally dictated to this
Prime Minifter, fhould be laid before him, for
his royal approbation; and the Minifter was to
make

make his report every week, what orders had been
issued from the cabinet, and deliver in an extract
of each of them; but *Struensee* took very little
notice of his Majesty's commands. He frequently
issued orders from the cabinet, without the King's
knowledge or permission, and even without make-
ing proper reports or extracts of them, as I shall
hereafter shew. In short, this presumptuous man
looked upon himself as the only person fit to be
intrusted with government, and on whom his Majesty's happiness, and the prosperity of Denmark
and Norway, solely depended. But to effectuate
this, every thing was to be new-modelled, it was
immaterial, what were the consequences of these
changes. It was *his pleasure*, and that was sufficient. The inhabitants of both kingdoms he considered as the savage natives of the forest, who
knew, not their own happiness. He therefore
thought it no crime to oppress them. His Majesty's servants and every one at court trembled
before him. His own servants he looked upon as
the most abject slaves: On their committing the
least fault, he reproached them, that they were
neither fit nor worthy to serve men of high rank,
whereby he meant his own person. Thus his
impudence betrayed his pride even in the minutest
actions. This ambitious man had forgotten his former condition and station in life, in which there are
certainly many very able and more experienced men
than himself, who are suffered to spend their lives
in obscurity. His passion and cruelty often carried him so far, that even in the King's presence,
(to whom he himself was a servant) he often
abused and treated his Majesty's domesticks in a
most cruel manner. His own words, in his answer to Count *Brandt's* admonishing letter, above-
mentioned,

mentioned, will beft prove his imperious and cruel difpofition. They are as follows.—" *Vous* " *me reprochez, que j'infpire la peur à tout le monde,* " *& vous m'en devez faire compliment, parceque* " *c'eft la feule refource pour un état énervé, affoiblie* " *avec une cour & tout un public intriguant, & un* " *maître ft—p—de & ig—r—t, & qui a le* " *même penchant pour le changement que fon peuple.*" (*) In another piace he exprefles himfelf thus :— " *La bonté & les complaifances, ont été la fource du* " *malheur de Dannemarc.*" (†) But why fhould we wonder, that he oppreffed a nation, whofe Monarch he dared to infult and abufe ?

One fhould have imagined, that ftate affairs might have fufficiently employed this man ; but he always continued to act as phyfician, and that (according to his own declaration) out of tendernefs to the Royal Family. His Royal Highnefs the Hereditary Prince of Denmark was to be educated according to his caprice. But no man of fenfe could conceive what views this Doctor had, in his method of educating this Prince; for it feemed, as if he intended to deprive him firft of his health and good conftitution, in order to fhew, that by his art he could give it him again. But this trial might have proved unfuccefsful and detrimental to the nation. Other perfons of the Royal Family, whom his fubtle arts and machinations could not blind, and who could fee into the Wickednefs of

his

(*) " You reproach me for what you ought to pay me a " compliment—that I appear dreadful to all that furround " me. It is the only refcource left to recover a ftate, weak-" ened and enervated by the intrigues both of the Public " and the Court, and by the ftu—p—y and ig—i—e of a " mafter, who, like his people, is as unfteady as the wind." (†) " Generofity and complaifance have been the caufes " of the misfortunes of Denmark."

his heart, were by him defpifed and trea ed in a moft unbecoming manner. Every member of this moft Honourable Court, knows, as well as myfelf, what grief and forrow it has caufed the whole nation, to fee his Majefty's own brother (who certainly is the King's beft friend) feparated and kept at a diftance from his Majefty, by the artful contrivances of *Struenfee* (*).

All his Majefty's former minifters of ftate, and many other perfons of the higheft rank and firft families in the kingdom, were, by this impireous minifter, treated with unbecoming indifference and haughtinefs, they therefore declined appearing at court, and retired to their country feats, or into foreign countries, by which Denmark, and particularly the city of Copenhagen, loft great part of its trade in the neceffary articles of life.

He not only interfered in matters of which he underftood nothing, but alfo always appointed people to fuch offices, and for the execution of fuch bufinefs, of which they had not the leaft knowledge; from whence every fenfible man concluded, that this mighty minifter meant to turn every thing into a chaos, and intended entirely to abolifh the ancient form of government, in order to fubftitute another, the infant of his own fancy.

The language and laws of the country he utterly, defpifed. Every thing was, according to his orders, to be tranflated into the german language.

(*) What the Danifh Attorney-General means here to hint at, is, that another box in the playhoufe was affigned to Prince Frederick, his Majefty's brother, whereas he formerly conftantly fat in the fame box with the King.

guage. This, in many respects, gave double trouble, and hindered the dispatch of business, notwithstanding he gave to all his actions the appearance of agility, and it seemed as if every thing should be executed with uncommon swiftness and dispatch.

He was no friend to the city of Copenhagen. He thought it too great, and too flourishing a town for Denmark. He therefore undertook to diminish its lustre and strength, by depriving its inhabitants of those privileges, which their forefathers had obtained as rewards for their loyalty, in defending their King and country at the hazard of their lives and fortunes. On the other part, he amused the vulgar with all kinds of fantastical innovations. All the laws established for the maintenance of decency and good manners were abolished, and licentiousness, and vices of every kind, were encouraged; insomuch that the lewdest libertine might gratify his most wanton appetite without fear of reprehension.—It would be too tedious to mention all the glaring absurdities committed by, or through the instigation of, this daring and audacious man. These infamous proceedings he affected to consider as very meritorious, and he firmly expected, that every one should consider him as *de Dania bene meritus.* He therefore could not persuade himself, that too great an honour had been conferred upon him, in creating him a Danish Count. His audacity appeared in all his actions. To think himself worthy of that dignity, because he had been two years in Denmark, to the utter mortification of its inhabitants, was consummate impudence! In former times, when any one was promoted to that exalted dignity, it was considered as a proof

of

of that perfon's merit and abilities; and as a reward for effential fervices rendered either to his
King or his country. But the contrary was here
the cafe. Count *Struenfee* viewed this matter in a
different light. He confidered, that what is called *rank* and *character*, as fomething, we need not
to feek for, nor ftrive to deferve by particular
fervices; but what muft abfolutely be given to
perfons of merit and abilities, as for inftance, to
his brother, who on account of his great know-
lege (or rather ignorance) of the finances of Denmark, was made a privy-counfellor. He concluded, therefore, that creating him a Danifh Count,
was not beftowing any particular favour upon him,
but that he had a right to that dignity, on account
of his merit and great abilities. The only mark of
humility he gave on that occafion, was, that he
fuffered his trufty friend *Brandt* to be raifed to
the fame dignity, though the latter had given
himfelf but little concern about ftate-matters,
and knew lefs of them than even *Struenfee* himfelf.—But as they could both fay: " *Vivimus ex*
" *rapto*," fo it was neceffary, that they fhould
fhare equally in honour, as well as in the booty.
However juft and innocent might be her Majefty's motives for inftituting the order of *Ma-
tilda*, it is certain that *Struenfee* (who feemingly
was the firft projector thereof, as he was almoft
the firft man that was invefted with that order)
had his fecret views, to obtain thereby the order
of the *Elephant*.

His impudence in this and many other circumftances, at laft debafed him fo much in the
eyes of every fenfible friend to his country, that
a general diffatisfaction was vifible on every
countenance. Wherever he appeared, he met

millions

millions of curses. The daily publications and
satires on Count *Struensee* and his party, which
were always well received by the populace, shewed the disposition of the nation, and their disgust
to all his proceedings. It was impossible for him
to remain ignorant of the prevailing sentiments
of the people. Many of his adherents, who before had officiously spread abroad their master's
merits and abilities, in representing to the com-
monality the many imaginary advantages that
would derive from all the different alterations and
new regulations in the kingdom, and who, together with their empirical doctor, were looked upon
as so many quacks and leeches, began to desert
him, when they saw the approaching danger,
and took shelter in foreign countries. Even his
friend *Brandt* (who perhaps may be pitied by
some people, but who, on account of his attachment to *Struensee*, and the crimes he committed, is in no degree excusable) seems to have
been sensible of the fatal consequences that would
follow, and warned and admonished him accordingly. These circumstances made him attentive,
and soon shewed his cowardly disposition. So
proud and audacious he had shewn himself in
his prosperity, so mean and dejected was he in
apparent danger (*.) He was like a man involved in a labyrinth, from which he can find no out-
let. The means he adopted to remedy the evil,
contributed to encrease it. His Majesty's horse-
guards

(*) Cicero lays it down as a certain maxim, that the man
who is insolent in prosperity will certainly be mean in ad-
versity. and hence it is that we frequently see the most
haughty and tyrannical ministers steal out of office, retire
to some solitary retreat, and there amidst horror, anguish,
and despair, linger out their wretched days in oblivion.

guards had been difmiffed, under the fpecious pretence that then maintainance was too weighty to be fupported. The foot-guards, which chiefly confifted of natives from both kingdoms, now became the object of his hatred. He knew their love and attachment to their fovereign, and therefore confidered them as the more dangerous to his own fecurity. They were accordingly difmiffed alfo, and in this affair he plainly acted as a traitor to his King and benefactor, which I fhall prove clearly hereafter. This, and many other new regulations, had no other effects, than to increafe the general diffatisfaction of the people. The inhabitants of Copenhagen, being forely weary of this doctor of phyfic, who had fo long been diffecting the laws and privileges of their country, now began to wifh for an opportunity to anatomife him in their turn, and, though they might not perform this operation to the fatisfaction of the faculty, yet they wifhed to attempt the work, as it would at leaft contribute to gratify the refentment of an injured and oppreffed people, and ferve as a memento to evil minifters in future times. The difturbance that happened on Chriftmas-eve, fufficiently fhewed, that every mind was ripe for open rebellion, which would probably have been the deftruction of many of our citizens, and deluged our ftreets with blood and flaughter, had not God, in his infinite wifdom, perverted the impending ftorm.

In this fituation Count *Struenfee* could not avoid feeing the evil effects of all his dark and wicked machinations. Though his guilty foul told him, that no good could await fuch actions, yet was he incapable of repenting; and,

like

like the angels of darkness, he determined to push forward, and fill up the measure of his iniquity. What were his views, may not be easy to conceive, but we need not hesitate a moment to pronounce them the offspring of mischief. Whenever his Majesty came to town, his passage through the streets of Copenhagen was so rapid, that he appeared more like a man who fled before his enemies, than a beloved Monarch who appeared amongst his faithful subjects. The cause of this conduct was easily seen into: It was the minister's interest to deprive the subject of every opportunity of approaching the ear of their sovereign, or of even presenting to him memorials, which might clear up his fight to take a just view of his situation (*). In short, these, and many other new regulations, which were made when the Court came to town from Friedrickſburg with different persons of the Royal Family, plainly evinced, that either the King was afraid of his subjects, or that Count *Struenſee* had resolved, (in case he could not discover any convenient method to get rid of his Majesty's person) to make him appear contemptible in the eyes of the people, and as unfit to wield the scepter of Denmark, and then to declare himself the *Protector* of both kingdoms.

To insinuate himself with the soldiers, who after the dismiffion of the body-guard, did duty in the palace, he ordered, that besides their usual pay, provisions should be provided for them

every

(*) It is not only in Denmark, but even in a more southerly kingdom, where the Monarch flies from one palace to another, as if he hated or dreaded the fight of his subjects.

every day, which had never before been cuftomary.

For his better fecurity in the city of Copenhagen, he appointed one of his adherents to the
place of Commander in chief of that city, who,
in every part of his conduct and behaviour, ri-
diculed the city on all occafions. The city gates
were ordered to be left open all night, in order
that thofe in the fuburbs, in cafe of an infurrec-
tion, might take fheltei in the city. A certain
number of cannon were ordered to be kept
loaded and in readinefs for immediate ufe. In a
word, fuch dreadful and warlike preparations
were made, as if we expected a powerful enemy
before the town, or as if his Majefty's faithful
fubjects, the inhabitants of Copenhagen, on the
leaft mark of diffatisfaction, were immediately
to be facrificed to the impudence, ambition, and
jealoufy of *Struenfee*. Every one knows, what
were our fears, terrors, and anxieties, as well
by night as day, to fee the end of all thefe proceedings, and to know what could be the defigns of the authors of them; though I believe,
and flatter myfelf with the pleafing idea, that
they would not have laid hands on the facred
perfon of his Majefty, and deprived him of his
life, fo long as they were permitted to act their
parts uninterrupted; yet fuppofing any infur-
rection had happened, not againft the King (for
every one is fully perfuaded of his fincere affection for his fubjects) but againft this daring and
audacious criminal—fuppofing the patience of
the nation had been exhaufted, and fome powerful friend to his country had undertaken to call
this traitor to account, the neceffary confequence
thereof, and the only means *Struenfee* and his

C 4

parts

party had left for their felf-prefervation, would
have been to attack and deftroy the King, in order that the higheft power might devolve to the
Queen, in which cafe he knew he was fecure
enough. What I mention here as a mere fup-
pofition, is however clearly the cafe, as may be
feen in his own letter to Count *Brandt*, now upon
the records before this Honourable Commiffion.

All thefe warlike preparations fufficiently
fhewed, that Count *Struenfee* was afraid of the
refentment of the populace, whom he had before affected to pleafe in every refpect, and this
is a proof that he was confcious of his bad actions. On the other hand, the diffatisfaction
the nation fhewed to all his proceedings, clearly
demonftrate their virtuous difpofitions, and fhews,
that though they fometimes may bear more than
other nations, they neverthelefs have a due veneration for the Almighty Being, a fincere affection for their King and country, and are ftrict
obfervers of decency and good manners. Our
prayers therefore afcended to Heaven and reached
the ear of him, by whom alone Monarchs govern. He heard our cries, and with a powerful
arm delivered us, in a moft miraculous manner,
from the mifery and ignominy which hung over
our country, our King, and the Royal Family :
the ever memorable 17th day of January was
the happy æra of our deliverance. The univerfal
joy, expreffed by all ranks of the people, fufficiently fhewed the general fatisfaction of that
happy event, from which Count *Struenfee* could
learn, " *quam caduca fit ifta felicitas.*"

For the fake of futurity, and in cafe this memorial fhould ever be read by others hereafter,
I find it neceffary to obferve, that all what I
have

have mentioned before, is but a ſhort abſtract of the facts, that have happened, but which, I hope, will be ſufficient to ſet the different crimes of Count *Struenſee* in their proper light. Neither do I wiſh to be conſidered as imprudent, if it ſhould appear, as though I had endeavoured to ridicule him on ſeveral occaſions, eſpecially in a memorial of accuſation in criminal matters, where the life of any man is depending, and where every thing ought be treated with the greateſt truth and ſolemnity; for there is a difference between an experienced miniſter of ſtate, who may have committed ſome faults, and an imperious quack doctor, who undertakes to manage the helm of government, and as ſuch ſhews himſelf the avowed enemy to his King and his country; beſides, many of Count *Struenſee*'s actions, which have in ſome meaſure an influence on his crimes, are in their nature ſo ridiculous, that it is impoſſible to repreſent them properly in any other light. But in order that Count *John Frederick Struenſee*, and every one whom it concerns, may be compleatly aſſured, that I have mentioned nothing, that might be called accuſations without proofs, I will here, purſuant to his Majeſty's moſt gracious commands, enumerate his different capital crimes, and authenticate them with the neceſſary proofs, which appear upon the records before this moſt Honourable Commiſſion. To enumerate all the crimes he has committed, would be as unneceſſary as impracticable, if we conſider that Count *Struenſee* has but one head to loſe, and when that is forfeited by one miſdemeanor, proofs beyond it are unneceſſary; though as many crimes might be proved againſt him as would juſtify his de-
capitation

capitation, even if he had as many heads as the Hydra. I therefore conclude this deduction with thefe words. " *Longa eft injuria, longæ ambages,* " *fed fumma fequar veftigia rerum.*"

I.

Count *John Frederick Struenfee* has committed a crime of high treafon, in that he, in a moft daring and audacious manner, has undertaken to feduce the firft Lady in the kingdom, whofe confidence he has obtained by the bafeft means, and extended the intimacy beyond the boundaries prefcribed by nature, law and decency, to perfons of different fexes, who cannot, and muft not be united. As I look upon this crime to be the greateft that can be committed by a fubject againft his fovereign, and as that which has precipitated Count *Struenfee* into all his other crimes, I therefore mention it the firft: and certainly it is a moft daring and unparalleled crime, and of which hiftory fcarcely furnifhes us with an example. I here refer the Honourable Judges to the different declarations of the witneffes upon oath, and particularly to that of her Majefty's maid of honour; not in order to prove what is fufficiently known, but to fhew, moft fubmiffively, that Count *Struenfee* has been the firft inftigator in this affair; that he, by his artifice and machinations has endeavoured to bring about this intimacy; that he has taken all meafures imaginable, to be made acquainted, and to be at hand, whenever an opportunity prefented itfelf, to fatisfy his impetuous and fhameful paffion; that the indifference with which he was treated at firft by that high perfon, whofe confidence he afterwards gained, fufficiently proves, that he was not led

into

into temptation by the victim of his brutality,
but that it was intirely his own inhuman audacity, his daring, subtle, and base intrigues,
which brought about this fatal intimacy, and involved a royal perfonage in a participation of
those crimes, which are forbidden by virtue,
dignity, education, and decency ; that for this
very reason he is the more punishable, as he has
endeavoured to raise himself into power and
places of honour, by bringing shame and ignominy on others. For the proofs of this most
horrid crime committed by Count *Struenfee*, I
refer this most Honourable Commission to
the following different proofs upon the records, viz.

1. To the first examination of both Counts,
Struenfee and *Brandt*, and Profeffor *Berger* (*fub
Lit.— p. —.*) (*) in which Count *Struenfee* has
indeed confeffed a particular intimacy and connection with the first Lady in the kingdom ; but
as he has laid every thing to her account,
and thinks both are excufable, particularly himfelf, as he had acted only in his medical
capacity ; and as there is no clear confeffion
of

(*) This and the following references point to the records, or original papers, which were laid before the Royal
Commission of Inquisition, and which contain the cross examination of the different witnesses. &c. None of them
have as yet tranfpired, and as they are very voluminous,
there is no probability they will ever be published, nor could
any great information be derived from them, since the Attorney-General has, in many places, given the subftance
of them. We have, however, let thefe references ftand
as we found them in the original, as they prove, that the
Attorney-General had particular authorities for what he
advances in thofe places.

of the fact, I need not examine this minute-
ly, nor feek for proofs in the anfwers of the
other two prifoners, as there are much bettei
proofs at hand. I therefore refer this Honourable Commiffion,

2. To Count *Struenfee*'s fourth examination,
(*fub Lit.* --- *p.* ---) where he, confcious of his
fins, and moved by a fenfe of his guilt, has openly
and freely confeffed this high crime, as committed by him, with all the circumftances and
informations neceffary. The Honourable Judges
have, in this important affair, required his fignature to this confeffion, with which he has freely
complied. I therefore refer,

3. To Count *John Frederick Struenfee*'s own free,
clear, and open confeffion of the perpetration of
this high crime, as figned and authenticated by
his own hand writing, (*fub Lit.* --- *p.* ---) further,

4. To her Majefty Queen C---ro---na M---
t---da's declaration of the truth of Count *Struenfee*'s confeffion, dated *Croneburgh, March* 4th, 1772.
(*fub Lit.* --- *p.* ---)

5. To Count *Enewold Brandt*'s declaration concerning the conferences he had with Count *Struenfee* on this affair, which proves the certain
knowledge he had of this horrid crime (*fub Lit.*
--- *p.* ---)

6 To profeffor *Berger*'s declartion, which corroborates in every refpect that of Count *Enewold
Brandt*. (*fub. Lit.* --- *p.* ---.)

7. To the declarations of her Majefty's maids
of honour, and their anfwers to the different
queftions during their examination. (*fub Lit.* ---
p. ---)

Befides all thefe inconteftible proofs, which
are more than fufficient for the prefent purpofe,
I could

I could refer this Honourable Committee to the declarations of many other witneffes, who have been examined upon oath, and which prove the audacious behaviour of this daring man; that he, without the leaft regard to decency, has purfued the moft wicked courfes, and, what is horrible to think of, not contented with feducing royal virtue, his conduct feemed to declare, that he wifhed to make her infamy known to the whole world. His continually running backwards and forwards; his abrupt entrance into the Queen's apartment, without being firft announced, even at unfeafonable hours; his long ftay there, his coaching and riding with her Majefty, even without any attendants, their frequent folitary walks in the gardens, his frequently giving and accepting prefents, and many other circumftances in the declarations of thefe witneffes, fufficiently corroborate the truth of his own confeffion, fo that he has by no means accufed himfelf wrongfully.

Count *Struenfee* has therefore been guilty of the crime of high treafon, and that in the moft aggravated light imaginable; he has openly and daringly violated the fidelity he owed his fovereign and royal mafter, and the refpect and veneration due to her Majefty. He has in a moft daring and audacious manner, wrefted from his royal mafter, that confidence, love, affection, and perfonal fecurity, to which his Majefty, after a folemn promife made in the prefence of God, had a fole and exclufive right. To arrive at dignities and power, he has facrificed the unblemifhed honour of the royal houfe, and loaded it with fhame and infamy. Where is the honeft man, however low and indigent he may be, who would not

think

think fuch treatment highly injurious to him?
—But how keen and humiliating is the thought,
that fuch an offence fhould be committed againft
the higheft perfons, againft the anointed of
God, againft the deareft objects of the nations
affections!—O the horrid deed, which even
the legiflator feems not to have forefeen, and
which cannot be mentioned with decency!—But,
if it is an offence againft the royal dignity to
cenfure the King or Queen for blameable actions,
it is a much greater crime to load thofe royal
perfonages with fhame and infamy. It is unneceffary for me to dwell any longer upon this fubject. The truth of the fact is fufficiently proved,
the confeffion of the crime cannot be denied,
and Count *Struenfee* may read his well merited
punifhment in the Danifh code of Laws, Book
VI. Chap. IV. Art. 1.

II.

Count *John Frederick Struenfee* was perfectly
well acquainted, that his Majefty ftood in danger of being affaulted and cruelly treated by
Count *Brandt*; and not only neglected to prevent this cruel deed, but even advifed and planned the whole tranfaction; and after this horrid
crime was perpetrated, fhewed his entire fatisfaction, and even promifed to reward the traitor
who had dared to commit that crime. In my
Memorial of Accufation, againft Count *Enewold
Brandt*, the Honourable Judges will fee the whole
proceedings in this affair, namely, that his Majefty was locked up in his own apartment by the
faid Count *Brandt*, who, after abufing the King
with fcandalous words, affaulted, beat, and bit
the King in fo cruel a manner, as admits of no

precedent

precedent. Hiſtory, as far as my knowledge reaches, furniſhes no example of ſuch an audacious action. We have, indeed, had inſtances of Kings being aſſaſſinated; but never that Kings had been chaſtiſed in ſo cruel and inſulting a manner, as would have been an affront to the meaneſt of his domeſtics. To ſhew, and to prove, that Count *Struenſee* not only had a previous knowledge of this affair, but that he even adviſed and approved of it, I ſhall refer this Honourable Commiſſion to the following inſtruments upon the records.

1. To Count *Enewold Brandt*'s declaration (*ſub Lit.* — *p.* —.) where he ſays, that after his Majeſty had been angry with him in the morning, and had threatened to cane him, he had conferred with *Struenſee* about this matter, who promiſed to talk with the King; that, on the afternoon of the ſame day, *Struenſee* came to *Brandt*, and ſaid to him: " I have
" opened this matter to the King, and he gave
" me for anſwer : *Brandt* is a coward; he has
" no courage; if he thinks himſelf affronted,
" let him come, I will give him ſatisfaction;
" I will fight with him, and make him ſubmit
" to his conqueror." — *Struenſee* continued :
" What will you do now? The beſt thing I
" can adviſe you, is to go to the King, and
" ſay to him : You have threatened to cane me,
" and I hear you will abſolutely fight with me;
" here I am now, if you dare to do the one or
" the other, then come on, and let us ſee who
" will get the beſt of it." Here *Struenſee* added,
" Such has often been the caſe with Count
" *Holck*, who, in order to keep the King in
" *due ſubjection*, has now and then been under
" the

" the neceffity of having recourfe to a few
" blows."

2. To Count *Brandt*'s further declaration
(*fub Lit.* — *p.* —) where he fays, that in the
evening, in which this affair had happened,
after he had left the King, he went to her Majefty's apartment, where he found *Struenfee* play-
ing at cards: When the party broke up, he
took *Struenfee* afide, and told him all that had
happened, upon which *Struenfee* gave him for
anfwer: " Now all will be right, and you will
" have peace, take my word for it; but take
" care that no one knows any thing of it."

3. To Count *Struenfee*'s own declaration
(*fub Lit.* — *p.* —) where he confeffes plainly, that he not only fpoke with Count *Brandt*,
concerning this affair, before it happened, but
alfo tha *Brandt* related to him the whole tranfaction, as foon as it was over.

Befides thefe fufficient proofs of the crime,
I could mention many other inftances, where
Count *Struenfee* himfelf has fet afide all due
refpect and veneration that are due from a fubject to his Sovereign; as, for inftance (*fub.
Lit.* — *p.* —) when his Majefty found his
prefcription fomewhat difagreeable or inconvenient, with regard to bathing, *Struenfee* faid:
" If he will not bathe, he may ....
" ....". I conclude, therefore, that Count *Struenfee*, as well as Count
Brandt, has in this affair committed the crime of
lefæ Majeftatis, as he was acceffary to it, knew
of it before it happened, not only neglected
preventing it, but gave his entire confent and
approbation to it, and even promifed rewards
for this and all other fuch proceedings, as appears

pears from his answer to Count *Brandt's* letter, where the latter mentions the hardship wherewith he finds himself necessitated to treat the King, *Struensee* expresses himself in the following words. " *La reconnoissance, que la Reine vous* " *aura, si vous reüssissiez, & les marques* " *incontestables que vous en avez déja reçu, vous* " *en recompenseront (*)*". Count *Struensee*, therefore also, in this respect, deserves to be punished, according to the Danish code of Laws, Book VI. Chap. iv. Art. 1 and 14.

III.

Count *John Frederick Struensee* has been guilty of the crime of high treason, in endangering the life of His Royal Highness the Hereditary Prince of Denmark, His Majesty's only son, the hopes and the joy of the nation; so that it plainly appears, that his wicked views were, either to make away with this young Prince, or at least to render him unfit for government. Besides all, what is sufficiently known, and to which many of the Honourable Judges, and several other persons, have been eye-witnesses, I refer this most Honourable Commission to the declarations of the different witnesses, who have been examined upon this affair, (*Lit.* —. *p.* — and *Lit.* — *p.* —) where we see with horror what cruelties this innocent Royal infant has undergone. Cold milk and water, raw fruits, and cold potatoes, were assigned for his Royal Highness,

---

(*) " The incontestible marks you have already received, " and the future acknowledgments of the Queen, if you " should at last succeed, will be an ample recompence."

nefs, as the moft nourifhing provifions. Whole
weeks have paffed, without his being permitted
to tafte any thing warm; for the leaft fault, he
was punifhed by being refufed to eat for the
whole day, which might have been productive of
the moft dangerous confequences in fo young and
tender a ftomach. During the whole winter,
and even in the fevereft froft, this Prince was left
alone, almoft half naked, and generally bare-
footed, in a cold room, without a fire, where
even the fervants could not poffibly bear the ri-
gour and feverity of the feafon. When in fuch
agonies, half-ftarved and frozen, the tender infant cried for help, the attendants had ftrict orders
not to affift him, and the Prince was left, for
hours together, to bewail his wretched fituation in
tears. I really believe, that had not the fervants,
moved by the tender feelings of humanity for this
innocent infant, broke through their orders in
many inftances, and warmed and nourifhed the
Prince, (for which even fome were difcharged)
it would have been impoffible for him to furvive
fuch cruel treatment. The proofs of all this
appear upon the records, as mentioned above,
and alfo, that all this treatment was by the abfolute command of this daring and audacious
Prime Minifter. Had he not found it an auxi-
liary to his private view, to retain the quality of a
phyfician; had he not advifed and ordered every
thing in this affair himfelf, it might have been
faid, in his excufe, that the education of the
Prince does not concern the Prime Minifter.
But fince his infatiable ambition to command as
abfolute mafter in every thing, led him even to
meddle with this bufinefs, he, as a phyfician,
fhould have known it to be impoffible to bring
up

up children in such a manner. I am fully convinced, that Count *Struensee* can produce no example of such a mode of education. He himself was not brought up in the like manner;
and yet the rotundity of his belly declares him to
be the *Vitellius* (*) of the present age. His views,

D 2

there-

(*) The Danish advocate here compares *Struensee* to
Vitellius The reader has seen part of the character of
Struensee, we will now give that of *Vitellius*, and leave the
world to judge of the similitude between them. " *Aulus
Vitellius*, who was proclaimed Emperor of Rome about the
sixty-ninth year of the Christian æra, was a monster of
cruelty. After the battle of Bebriacum, he delayed his
stay at that place, with no other view, than that he might
feast his brutal eves with the scattered and mangled limbs
of the slain, with the sight of the earth still reeking with
human blood, and, in short, with such a spectacle as in
every bosom, not totally callous to humanity, at once ex-
cites horror and pity. The pleasure he received from this
inhuman scene, overpowered every other feeling, insomuch
that he perceived not the infection of the air from the un-
burried dead. When his military companions, less savage
than himself, complained of their infectious situation, he re-
plied. " The fragrance of a dead enemy is always
" agreeable." He immediately ordered wine to be distributed among his soldiers, and the Emperor and his army
were companions in drunkenness. It appeared to him, that
the Imperial dignity consisted only in gluttony, and he
even contracted the habit of encouraging the motions which
nature kindly makes to relieve an overloaded stomach. He
caused his mother, *Sextilia*, to die with hunger, because it
had been predicted, that his reign would be long if he sur-
vived her. *Vitellius* having now filled the measure of his
iniquities, both the army and people arose against him,
and elected *Vespasian*. This monster was dragged from a
kennel of hounds, among whom he endeavoured to conceal
himself, and was led naked through the city, his hands
bound behind him, and a sword placed under his chin, to
make him walk erect. He was then led to the place of
execution, and there put to death by protracted tortures,
after having reigned eight months. His body was afterwards dragged away by a hook, and thrown into the
Tiber." *Nouv. Diction. Histor. Tom.* V.

therefore, in treating this young Prince in so cruel a manner, must either have proceeded from some iniquitous design he had upon him, to make away with him, or at least to ruin his intellectual faculties, and render him unfit for the high dignity he is by God and nature destined to, or else to make the dangerous trial of what effects such an education might produce; but in both cases he has committed High Treason; for his Royal Highness is not to be considered as a proper object for physical experiments. The allegation, with which Count *Struensee* endeavours to palliate this atrocious crime, by referring to the œconomy of brutes, is very foreign to the present case. Animals rear their young in a more tender manner, than *Struensee* prescribed for this Prince, and in this respect, his feelings were much inferior to those of a brute. There is a medium between a too tender, and too rigorous education. It is one extreme, not to suffer the least fresh air to blow upon children, and to feed them with nothing but light and luxurious dainties; and it is another extreme to starve and freeze them almost to death, and to give them nothing but raw and coarse food, unfit for their tender stomachs to digest. Therefore, as Count *Struensee* pretends to have some skill in his art, as a physician, he must have been sensible, that it was impossible for this royal infant to subsist any length of time under his cruel prescriptions; consequently his views in this affair must have been the very worst that can be thought of; and I may add, that it is owing only to the gracious protection of the Almighty, that the Prince is still living. But I am of opinion, that he, who causes the life of a Prince to be in danger, is as culpable as he

who

who attempts to deprive him of it; and that he also deserves to be punished, according to the Danish code of Laws, Book VI. Chap. iv. Art. 1.

IV.

Count *John Frederick Struensee* has grosly insulted the dignity of the King, and committed the crime of high treason, in that he has endeavoured, in a surreptitious manner, to obtain and execute the highest power, by signing orders from the cabinet with his own hand, instead of his Majesty's,—a power, which according to the constitution of this country, is only vested in the sovereigns of the realm, and cannot be executed by a subject. Count *Struensee*'s bad designs upon the King and the nation, are particularly conspicuous in this important affair, though he endeavours to alledge the most innocent motives for such conduct. His excuse, that having aimed at nothing else, than to promote the happiness of his Majesty, and the welfare of his subjects, and that he could see no harm in assuming this power, is soon defeated, when we reflect upon the consequences that have resulted from it. For, in the first place, instead of promoting the welfare of the subjects, the misery of the nation has daily increased under his government: And secondly, it is incredible that a man, who never had the least knowledge of state affairs, a man, who has no religion, whose daring ambition cannot listen to any subordination, who is a voluptuary in the highest degree, and consequently can have nothing more in view than the gratification of his unbounded appetites, —that such a man can perfect himself in the

course

course of two years, so as to undertake the government of two kingdoms; that he should be
confidered as the moft honeft man in the country,
and as one who cannot err, and who alone can
promote the happinefs and welfare of both the
King and the nation .—I fay it is incredible, and
no one would ever have imagined, that any perfon would attempt fuch a thing, if we had not
the proofs before our eyes.

This daring Count, who confidered himfelf
endowed with every good and amiable qualifi-
cation, has committed fuch atrocious crimes,
as will ever hold his memory in horror, even
with the very loweft clafs of the people, who
have but a very fuperficial idea of good manners, and of the veneration which is due from a
fubject to a fovereign. For it is certain, that
fuch barefaced and enormous crimes, committed
before the eyes of all the world, and without
the leaft regard to decency and good manners,
fuch as robbing his royal mafter, feducing his
royal confort, bringing fhame and infamy upon
the royal family, &c. &c. &c. muft fill every
one with horror and deteftation of the wretch
who committed them. And can there be any
excufe for the man, who, under the mafk of
friendfhip, under affurances of fidelity and fincere inclinations for the welfare of the ftate, under the appearances of difintereftednefs with regard to himfelf, and under the fpecious pretence
of faving the royal treafures, endeavours to em-
bezzle every thing, abufes the confidence of his
royal mafter, affumes in a furreptitious manner
the higheft power, and governs, inftead of the
King with unlimitted fway, in order to give to
his villainies a fplendid and brilliant appearance?

Count

Count *Struenſee* pretends, that the diſſolution of his Majeſty's Privy Council was the King's own project, becauſe his Majeſty was diſſatisfied with their manner and delays in executing all ſtate buſineſs ; with the heavy debts in which the ſtate was involved, and with the conſtraint he was generally put under in his Privy Council, to give up his opinion ; and that therefore he, *Struenſee*, could not oppoſe his Majeſty in this his royal will and pleaſure.---But this excuſe is as idle and ill-founded as the reſt. For let us ſuppoſe for a moment, that this had been his Majeſty's own pleaſure, (which it is evident it was not, ſince the ſame Privy Council is again eſtabliſhed) Count *Struenſee* could certainly not have oppoſed himſelf, with any degree of propriety, to his Majeſty's royal will and pleaſure ; but it was his duty, as a good ſubject, moſt ſubmiſſively to repreſent to his royal maſter : *firſt*, That ſince his Majeſty had but lately aſcended the throne, and taken the reins of government, he would certainly ſtand in need of able counſellors, to guide him through the difficult labyrinth of government ; *ſecondly*, That if there were any in his Majeſty's Privy Council, in whom his Majeſty could not confide, that other able men might be put in their places ; *thirdly*, That though a King of Denmark is under no obligations to have counſellors, or to regulate himſelf to the will of others, yet it redounds to his honour and intereſt to profit by the advice of wiſe and experienced men ; and, *fourthly*, That he, *Struenſee*, being bred to the ſtudy of phyſic, could know nothing of ſtate matters, of which, indeed, he was totally ignorant. Every one knows, that his Majeſty cannot bear flattery nor hypocriſy,

and

and therefore there is no doubt, that a Remonftrance of thefe motives, made in refpectful terms,
in a becoming and fubmiffive manner, would
have had the defired effect with the monarch.
But fo far from adopting thefe meafures, Count
Struenfee was fo audacious as to take upon himfelf that weighty bufinefs, which had before
given full employment to many experienced
ftatefmen; juft as if the art of government, and
the knowledge of the natural and commercial
interefts of two extenfive kingdoms, were to be
acquired by finging and dancing about the palace.

In my hiftorical introduction, I have fhewn in
what furreptitious a manner he obtained his Majefty's moft gracious order from the cabinet, of
July 14, 1774, which was communicated to
the different departments, and whereby he was
appointed Prime Minifter, with almoft equal
power to that of his Majefty. Though it had the
appearance as if, notwithftanding, every thing
depended upon his Majefty's approbation; yet, if
we confider this claufe properly, we fhall find it
to be a mere fallacy; for, as all bufinefs in the
cabinet was to be tranfacted by Count *Struenfee*,
and as his orders and refolutions were to have
the fame validity as thofe of the King, it is clear,
that whenever any thing was defpatched from
the cabinet, either prejudicial to the nation, or
contrary to former royal refolutions, and which
was returned to the cabinet with due remonftrances for alteration, in thefe cafes he always
became both judge and party himfelf. And
what fecurity had either the King or the nation,
that this mighty Prime Minifter would not injure the one or the other, fince he had the power

to examine, to alter, or to affirm, what he had once refolved upon ? Count *Struenfee*, when he firft had the good fortune and honour to come to the Court of Denmark, muft have certainly confidered the Danes and Norwegians as the moft abject flaves, who were to pay implicit obedience to all his orders and refolutions from the cabinet, without the leaft mark of difapprobation ; for, otherwife, it is impoffible to account for his audacity. Whoever undertakes to govern an empire in the place and in the name of the King, ought to be thoroughly acquainted with the reciprocal duties that fubfift between the King and his fubjects. Count *Struenfee* might have learned this from the Danifh and Norwegian code of Laws, Book I. Chap. 1. as alfo from the crown law, which was figned on Nov. 4, 1665, by King Frederick III. of glorious memory, and which fufficiently expreffes, that no defpotifm, but fovereignty only, belongs to the King. And whoever fhall advife to alter this law, is a traitor to the country, to the King, and to the fubjects ; and whoever fhall endeavour to perfuade the King, that his Majefty can alter or annihilate this law, is a contemptuous, wicked and profligate wretch.

This law of the empire, to which Kings are equally fubject, and which is a *conditio fine qua non* between them and their fubjects, cannot be altered by the fovereigns of thefe realms without the confent of the people, the nobility, and the clergy, unlefs their power and fovereignty be at the fame time annihilated or limitted. This law (Chap. iii.) exprefly orders, (for King Frederick III. as *primus acquirens* had a right to bind his fucceffors) that the fovereigns of this realm fhall

make

make no alterations whatfoever in this law; that they fhall derive their right of fucceffion to the crown no otherwife than according to this law; and that it fhall remain an unalterable bafis and fundamental law for both kingdoms. This law farther ordains: (Art. 7.) " That all concerns " of the empire, records, charters, edicts, and " all ftate bufinefs, fhall be tranfacted and iffued " in the King's name only, and under his feal, " and that he (if of age) fhall always authen- " ticate them with his own fignature." It far- ther ordains in the fevereft terms: (Art. 26.) " That in cafe any one, whofoever he may be, " fhall in any manner attempt to obtain or exe- " cute the power, vefted in the fovereign only, " and thereby endeavour to equal, diminifh, or " annoy, the King's prerogative, fhall, notwith- " ftanding all and every thing that might have " been faid, promifed, or obtained, be confi- " dered as of no effect, in any manner whatever, " and that he, who by his artifices has attempted " fuch things, fhall be confidered as a traitor to " his King, and his crime be deemed high " treafon againft the fole fovereign power of the " monarch, and he be punifhed accordingly."

Had Count *Struenfee* really not known this fun- damental law of the empire, though he under- took to govern alone both kingdoms, a houfe of correction, the habitation of lunatics, or the pillory, might have made fome atonement for his confummate arrogance; but fince he has con- feffed that he knew the contents of this law, but believed it was of no great fignification to affume and execute royal authority, he has, therefore, committed the crime of high treafon, and de- ferves to be punifhed accordingly.

V. If

V.

If we could fuppofe Count *Struenfee* excufeable for his having affumed the royal authority, contrary to thefe fundamental laws of the empire, he would ftill remain culpaple, for not having obeyed the inftructions laid down for his conduct in his Majefty's order, under the 14th of July, 1771, wheieby he obtained this power. This plainly fhews, that his views, in endeavouring to obtain this power, were not to eafe his Majefty of the burthen of government; but only to play more effectually the part he had piopofed for the better fecurity of himfelf and his adherents. But it would be unnceceffary, as well as tedious, to mention here all the intrigues he put in practice for that purpofe, and all the inftances, in which he has acted contrary to his Majefty's particular orders. One example will be fufficient; and in cafe Count *Struenfee* fhould not think his criminality fufficiently proved, I have many more at his fervice.

Count *Struenfee* had been the caufe of the difcharge of his Majefty's horfe-guard. The footguard had alfo become an object of his hatred, and he refolved to free himfelf from them likewife. The whole affair was nearly thus connected: Count *Struenfee* was afraid that his wicked actions might foon or late meet with their due reward, and fince he could expect no happy iffue, he thought of means to provide for his own fecurity. The life-guard, which confifted intirely of natives of Denmark and Norway, whofe love and attachment to their King and the Royal Family have always proved unalienable, was a fecure fence around the royal houfe, and confequently thorns in the eyes of *Struenfee*. He
therefore

therefore thought it neceſſary to remove theſe obſtacles to his future views. On December 21, 1771, he iſſued an order from the cabinet, unknown to the King, purporting the diſbanding of his Majeſty's foot or body-guard, with inſtructions to incorporate them with other regiments, The reaſon he gave, was to make an equality amongſt the officers as well as common ſoldiers, becauſe they all ſerved one and the ſame King. The true cauſe however was, that the Count knew he had no friends in the bodyguard, and in caſe of an unlucky accident, they, to a man, would have been the firſt perſons ready and willing to ſecure him. As ſoon as this order was known, and the guard refuſed to yield obedience, and to be incorporated among the other Regiments where *Struenſee*'s creatures commanded, he obtained, under falſe pretences, his Majeſty's ſignature to another order from the cabinet, purporting : that, " Whereas the guard " refuſed to do duty in the royal palace in com- " pany with the grenadiers of other Regiments, " his Majeſty was graciouſly pleaſed to grant " a diſcharge to all officers and common ſoldiers " of his body-guard, who would no longer re- " main in his ſervice." The daring audacity and wicked machinations of Count *Struenſee* in this affair, will appear more ſtriking, if we conſider the following points :

1. His Majeſty was entirely unacquainted with the diſmiſſion of his body-guard, in the manner as it is above related ; and as this corps has ſince that time been re-eſtabliſhed, it is a certain proof, that it was not diſbanded by his Majeſty's will and command.

2. His

2. His Majesty had not signed the order of December 21, when issued from the cabinet.

3. When Count *Struensee* obtained his Majesty's approbation for disbanding the body-guards, it was in consequence of his representing to the King, that the guards refused to do duty in the palace with the other grenadiers, which was an absolute falsity, for they only refused to be incorporated with other regiments.

4 Notwithstanding there were several orders, from the 21st till the 24th of December, ready for his Majesty's approbation, Count *Struensee* did not lay them before the King, and for this reason, that by the approbation of the second order, he might obtain the same to the first, which was dated December 21.

He has therefore also, in his employment as Prime Minister, been guilty of the highest misdemeanor, in issuing false orders from the cabinet, without any knowledge, or instruction from the King, of which more instances appear upon the records (*sub Lit. — p. —*) and he has also, in this respect, committed the crime of High Treason, according to the Danish code of Laws, Book I. Chap. i. Art. 1.

VI.

Count *John Frederick Struensee*, after having obtained full power over the treasury, has defrauded it of many considerable sums, the proofs of which appear upon the records (*sub Lit. — p. —*) It would be too tedious to mention all his frauds and embezzlements, I shall therefore confine myself to the most material only; and Count *Struensee* cannot complain of injustice, if I do not enumerate

enumerate all his misdemeanors, especially as they are innumerable.

The first grasp he made into the royal coffers, was the sum of 10,000 rixdollars, (*record Lit. — p. —*) Soon after which he accepted 3000 dollars for his new-year's gift, and to Count *Brandt*, in order to keep him silent and true to his interest, he procured the like sum of 3000 dollars. To the countess of *Holstein*, for reasons best known to himself, another like sum of 3000 dollars, because she had lost her money at the gaming-tables, as if the nation was obliged to support the countess in her luxury and dissipation. One present followed another, to the partisans of his iniquity, and among others, in particular, to colonel Falkenschiold, the sheet anchor, to which *Struensee* had fastened the crazy vessel of his hopes. Many considerable sums he procured from the royal treasury for his brother, under pretence that a financier must have money in his hands, in order that he may not be tempted to rob the revenue.— From this very maxim of procuring money for his brother, in order to hinder him from embezzling, we may infer what was the honesty of *Struensee*, who had no such agent to procure him money, with a view to keep him from stealing. No wonder, therefore, that *Struensee* has been as great a plunderer as ever decorated any fatal tree since gibbets were invented, as is plainly proved in many instances upon the records before this most Honourable Commission, and will appear more clearly, by the following forgery.

Soon after *Struensee* had thus provided for himself and his trusty friends, as above-mentioned, fresh sums of money were received in the treasury, over which he found himself *plenum dominum.*

num. Struenſee, not conſidering the exigency of the ſtate, had now nothing more at heart, than to procure freſh ſupplies for himſelf and his friends. He watched the opportunity of his Majeſty's good humour, and then ſolicited freſh preſents for himſelf and his dependants. He included in his liſt of ſolicitations, a high lady, who certainly did not ſtand in need of his interceſſion, ſince ſhe was always amply provided for, and therefore this could be from no other motive than ſelf-intereſt, and in hopes that the King would more readily acquieſce with his requeſts. His Majeſty was accordingly, in his royal bounty, pleaſed to grant to his royal conſort, the ſum of 10000 rixdollars, and to both Counts *Brandt* and *Struenſee,* 6000 rixdollars each. But Count *Struenſee,* who looked upon 6000 dollars as a trifle, and who had full power over his Majeſty's coffers, ſoon found means to increaſe that ſum. To give a greater ſanction to his intended fraud, he prepared with his own hand, an inſtrument for the grant of theſe preſents, ſpecifying the above-mentioned ſums in the following manner, and laid it before his Majeſty for his royal approbation, *viz.*

To her Majeſty	-	10000 Rixdollars.
To Count *Brandt*	-	6000
To Count *Struenſee*	-	6000

Total 22000 Rixdollars.

After having obtained his Majeſty's ſignature to the inſtrument, he added a nullo to both the ſums mentioned after Count *Brandt*'s and his own name, and thus changed them both from 6000 into 60000; the produce of which, together with

with 10000 for her Majesty, made 130000.
This sum being difficult to substitute in the room
of the original sum 22000, without too apparent
an alteration, for *Struenfee* conceived, that it was
easy to prefix a figure of 1 before the first figure of
2 ; then adding a small stroke under the first figure
of 2, and so changing it into a 3, which would
have produced the sum of 132000. In order
therefore to avoid scratching and altering the second figure of 2, in the original instrument of
the grant, he added a present of 2000 dollars for
his friend Falkenschiold, whose name and sum,
from the difference in the writing, clearly appears
to have been added, after the line over the total
produce, was drawn in the the original instrument, which appears now thus:

To Her Majesty   -   10000 Rixdollars.

To Count *Brandt*   -   60000

To Count *Struenfee* -   60000
To Colonel Falkenschiold   2000

Total 132000 Rixdollars.

Whoever closely examines this original instrument will soon perceive, that the two nullo's
have been added, and that the sums of 6000 have
been changed into 60000 ; likewise, that the first
figure of 2 has been changed into a 3 ; and both
Counts *Struenfee* and *Brandt* have themselves confessed that it has all the appearance of having
been forged. But to prove that it is a certain
and undeniable fraud, I beg leave here to observe
that,

1. His

1. His Majesty has positively declared, that he has never made them a present of 60000 Rixdollars at one time.

2. It appears strange and improbable, that his Majesty should, at one and the same time, have presented two of his subjects with 60000 Rixdollars each, and his royal consort with only 10000.

3. All the excuses which Count *Struensee* alledges for his exculpation in this affair, are invalidated by what appears upon the records (*Lit.* — *p* —) and by a close inspection of the original instrument.

Count *Struensee* has, therefore, in this affair, not only committed a forgery, but also robbed his Majesty's treasures of considerable sums, and thereby committed the crime of high treason, according to the Danish code of Law, Book I. Chap. i. Art. 10.

VII.

Count *Struensee* knew of, advised, and assisted, in the disposal of her Majesty's superb diamond nosegay, which was valued at above 40000 Rixdollars, though known to be of much greater worth. This precious piece of jewels was sent to the state counsellor *Waitz*, at Hamburgh, with commission to sell it for 10000 Rixdollars, notwithstanding he very well knew that it was part of her Majesty's ornaments, the property of the crown, and of which no reigning queen of this kingdom should be deprived, as may be further seen by what appears upon the records (*Lit.* — *p.* —)

Count *Struensee* has therefore also in this point, acted like a fraudulent traitor to his King, not

E   only

only in caufing fuch valuable jewels to be fold at
fo fhameful a rate ; but alfo, becaufe there was
no neceffity for difpofing of them, to the indelible difgrace of their owner.

VIII.

In order that this affair, as well as the robberies
he committed on the treafury, and all his other
wicked intrigues and artful machinations, might
not come to the knowledge of his royal mafter :
he gave orders, that all letters and other writings
directed to his Majefty, fhould for the future be
delivered into the Cabinet, fo that he might be
the firft acquainted with their contents, and in
cafe of any information to his difadvantage, might
adopt fuch meafures, as he fhould think moft
proper for his defence, fecurity, or the execution of his infernal defigns. (*Lit.* --- *p.* ---)

IX.

At laft, when Count *Struenfee* perceived he
had reached the precipice of ambition, he began to look down from its fummit with horror
and dread ; he fhuddered at his prefent fituation,
which was lefs dreadful, if poffible, than his
defpair of making good his afcent. He endeavoured to confole himfelf with reflecting, that
thofe whom he moft dreaded, were either removed, or as he thought, rendered incapable
of hurting him. The Burghers and others,
who compofed the corporation of Copenhagen,
were ftill an object of his attention , but thefe
he hoped to keep in awe, by appointing one of
his adherents to the place of commander in chief
of the city, and ordering that cannon (as I
have before-mentioned) fhould be kept loaded.

and

and in readiness for immediate service. Count *Struenfee*, indeed, denies his giving immediate orders for that purpose; and says, that it was only by way of conversation between him and Major General *Gude*, when he expressed his wish, that every thing, that was necessary for the maintainance of good order, might be kept in constant readiness. But when we consider, that there have always been proper regulations in Copenhagen for that purpose, we shall soon find the futility of this extraordinary precaution, which must have either proceeded from a motive of fear, that he should meet with no agreeable recompence for his wicked actions; or from an intent to execute some secret scheme of his own invention. For, if we closely consider what appears upon the records (*Lit. — p. —*) we shall soon be convinced, that his design was, in case he could not defend himself and maintain his ground any longer, he would have decamped, and taken a *certain person* with him.

I am therefore fully persuaded, that from what I have here mentioned, and authenticated by such undeniable proofs as appear upon the records before this most Honourable Court, it is clearly proved, that Count *Struenfee* has in many instances committed the crime of high treason in the highest degree possible to conceive, against the Majesty of the King, the Royal Family, and both nations at large. I am consequently of opinion, that Count *John Frederick Struenfee,* for his different crimes, deserves this sentence:

" That he be degraded from his dignity as Count;
    " that he has forfeited his honour, his life and
    " his property, and that his coat of arms be
    " broken by the common hangman; that his

" right

" right hand, and afterwards his head be
" cut off, and his body quartered and laid
" upon the wheel, and his head and hand
" ftuck upon a pole; that his eftates fhall
" be confifcated for the crown, and his
" heirs, if there be any, forfeit their rank
" and titles."

And thus, I humbly fubmit thefe indubitable facts to the wife, impartial, and fuperior judgement of this moft Honourable Commiffion.

Copenhagen,
April 20, 1771.

F. W. Wivet.

12 JY 62

T H E

THE

MEMORIAL of DEFENCE,

IN BEHALF OF

COUNT JOHN FRED. STRUENSEE,

AGAINST

The Accusations of the Attorney General.

LAID BEFORE THE

ROYAL COMMISSION of INQUISITION,

At COPENHAGEN, April 22, 1772,

By N. UHLDAL,

Attorney in His MAJESTY's higheft Court of Judicature.

T H E

Memorial of Defence, &c.

MY LORDS,

HIS Majefty having been moft gracioufly pleafed to command me, on the 23d of March laft, to undertake the defence of Count *John Frederick Struenfee,* according to the true tenor of the law, I will endeavour to fulfil this duty to the beft of my abilities, and with all the moderation and refpect that is due from the Count to his judges.

Among the many misfortunes that furround him at prefent, there is one circumftance the more aggravating, as it is the leaft expected: that is, the contempt and ridicule the Attorney-General has thrown upon all his actions. To aggravate circumftances to the injury of the accufed, is indeed a very unnatural but common confequence of his unhappy fituation; but that his private circumftances, his origin, his former condition and employment of life, his manner

of

of thinking, &c. that thefe fhould have been expofed to the mockery of his accufer, is an addition to his mifery, from which he thought himfelf fecure, if not from a motive of compaffion to his prefent misfortunes, yet at leaft, on account of the favour and affection wherewith his Majefty has condefcended to honour him, and the approbation the King has always given to his political principles, agreeable to which he has acted.

There is fcarcely a circumftance, however indifferent and trifling, but what the Attorney-General makes ufe of to blacken the character of the Count in the eyes of his judges. He is called a foreigner, though on the promotion of his father in the dukedom of Holftein, he became a fubject of this country in his infancy. That he was not perfect mafter of the Danifh language, was certainly a defect in him; but the fame has been the cafe with many preceding Minifters of ftate, and yet their ignorance in this refpect has never been conftrued a crime of high treafon.

If he has had fome fhare in the orders from the cabinet which fuppreffed fome public characters, and tended to the reduction of placemen and penfioners, I am fully perfuaded, that no friend to this country has as yet denied the neceffity and utility of fuch a meafure. And if the title or character of a counfellor of ftate was not, in the Attorney-General's opinion becoming a mathematician, fuch as the Count's brother, it is a fault which cannot be laid to the charge of Count *Struenfee*, becaufe his brother had the title of a counfellor long before he came to Denmark. His religion, the only fource of comfort in his

prefent

preſent misfortunes, is even denied him. His manner of thinking, all his actions, the minuteſt of
his failings, in ſhort, every thing is turned into
ridicule. It would be too tedious for me to examine every thing of that kind, which the Attorney-General mentions in his memorial of accuſation. Every one knows, that the method of prov-
ing a man guilty of certain crimes, by turning
his actions into ridicule, and making him appear odious, is not concluſive: ſince an ingenious
ſatiriſt may turn the moſt ſerious ſubjects into objects of laughter and contempt. Beſides, the
greateſt part of what the Attorney-General, in
his hiſtorical introduction, reproaches the Count
with, are objects quite foreign to the preſent caſe,
and do not belong to thoſe which, according to
his Majeſty's commands, are to be diſcuſſed before this moſt Honourable Commiſſion.

The matter here in queſtion is, to examine
what crimes Count *Struenſee* has committed againſt
the law and conſtitution of the country and the
Majeſty of the King. Of theſe he is to be ac-
cuſed; againſt this accuſation I am ordered to defend him, and of the importance and validity of
theſe crimes, this moſt Honourable Commiſſion is appointed to judge.—The Attorney-General has enu-
merated Count *Struenſee*'s tranſgreſſions in nine different ſections, which, according to his opinion,
conſtitute as many crimes of high treaſon. But as
they are all deemed offences either againſt the conſtitution of the ſtate, the form of government and
its adminiſtration, or againſt the perſon of his
Majeſty and the Royal Family: I ſhall direct this
memorial of defence to theſe two principal points,
and diſcuſs each of them ſeparately.

The

What in regard to the firſt point is laid to the charge of Count *Struenſee*, is the order from the cabinet of July 14, 1771, and the power he thereby received. To ſhew his audacity in this affair, the Attorney-General makes uſe of two arguments : *Firſt*, the aſſurance of Count *Struenſee*, as a phyſician, to meddle with ſtate affairs, and diſmiſſing his Majeſty's Privy Council, of which, ſays he, a confuſion in every department of government, the loſs of ſeveral able ſtateſmen, an oppreſſion of the nobility and the nation at large, and the decline of the capital, have been the unhappy conſequences. *Secondly*, That the power Count *Struenſee* thereby obtained, approached that of royal authority, becauſe he reſolved, ordered, and ſigned inſtead of the King ; and whenever any remonſtrances againſt any of his ordonnances came to the cabinet, it depended intirely on him, either to lay them before his Majeſty, or ſuppreſs them, and command obedience to his firſt orders ; all which, the Attorney-General endeavours to perſuade you is againſt the Law, Cap. III. Art. 7. and 26. where the aſſuming of ſuch a power is declared a crime of high treaſon.

Upon the whole, it appears to me, that the firſt of theſe arguments has no connection at all with the matter the Attorney-General was ordered to diſcuſs, and on which this Honourable Commiſſion is appointed finally to determine ; for, ſince Count *Struenſee* derived his influence in ſtate affairs, ſolely from the King; and as *Struenſee*'s actions were only the reſult of his Majeſty's will and pleaſure, nothing in this reſpect can be laid to the Count's charge, becauſe all conſequences muſt neceſſarily revert upon the King himſelf. To examine whether Count *Struenſee*, in obedience to the

King's

King's commands, has advifed or affifted him in ftate affairs, and what have been the confequences of the Count's advices, is in fact nothing elfe, than fcrutinizing the conduct of his Majefty in the government of his kingdoms, and as this is not in the power of any fubject to do, Count *Struenfee* can by no means be made accountable for any advice he gave his Majefty, and which the King has fealed with his approbation. I therefore am not able to difcover, in any part of this charge, the leaft proof of criminality. It is true, that Count *Struenfee*'s origin and former fituation in life, could give him but little hopes of the high dignities he afterwards obtained ; but with how many examples does hiftory furnifh us, of men of low extraction having been raifed to the higheft dignities : And as his Majefty thought him worthy of fuch dignities, had he not a right to accept of them ? Or is his Majefty, in the difpofal of his favours, fubject to the controul of his fervants ?

The Privy Council was never confidered as an effential part in the Danifh conftitution. That his Majefty had long been difpleafed with the manner of executing bufinefs in that affembly, appears plainly from many inftances mentioned upon the records before this Moft Honourable Court, and particularly (*Lit.* — *p.* —) And the beft proof of this that can be given, is, that His Majefty, with his own hand, wrote the order for the diffolution of this Council. Let us fuppofe alfo, that Count *Struenfee* advifed this meafure : We find in many places upon the records, and particularly in Count *Brandt*'s declaration (*Lit.* — *p.* —) that many perfons were of the fame opinion, and advifed the fame operations ; and as the new plan for the execution of all ftate bufi-

nefs

nefs was fuch, that the chief officers of the different departments fhould, in all occurrences falling unde their cognizance, be allowed to give their opinion, but that none but his Majefty fhould finally decide in all affairs, it cannot be faid, that the King's authority has in any refpect been either extended, or limited, more than was authorifed by the conftitution of the country.—That the ftate bufinefs, fince the diffolution of the Privy Council, has not been executed with the fame diligence and punctuality, or that the nation had been uncommonly opprefled by the promotion of fome foreigners are affertions without proofs, for nothing of that appears upon the records, nor can experience induce us to believe it. None of the nobility have been forbidden the court, except the Count *Laurwig*, who, for reafons well known, had once before incurred the like difgrace; and if fome have retired to their country feats, and the city of Copenhagen has thereby fuffered a decline in its trade, it may be attributed more to the exigency of the times, than to other caufes. Should this point undergo a political difcuffion, it would plainly appear, that the welfare of the empire is by no means promoted in the greatnefs and luxury of its capital, the high price of provifions, and magnificence of its buildings. I am fully perfuaded, that when King Frederick IV. impofed a double duty on the different articles confumed in the city of Copenhagen, his views were not fo much to augment his revenue, as to prevent the too great increafe of the capital, which at laft would have engroffed all trade and bufinefs, to the great prejudice of every other town in both kingdoms. England and France have long complained, that

their

their capitals infenfibly fwallowed up every thing
the fertility of their climates, or the induftry
of their inhabitants, were able to produce; and
experience has fhewn, that the celebrated *Duke*
of Sully judged very judicioufly, when, to correct
this evil, he wifhed that thofe of the French nobility, who have no concerns in public or ftate
bufinefs, would live prudently on their eftates in
the country, and encourage and affift their tenants
in their different occupations, rather than fpend
their days amidft the follies, luxuries, and diffi-
pations of the capital, which generally brought
ruin on themfelves and their families.

What the Attorney-General, in his *fecond* argument, lays to the charge of Count *Struenfee*, is
the power he obtained by the ordonnance of July
14, 1771. It cannot be denied, that it depended
entirely upon His Majefty himfelf, whom he
would deign worthy his confidence, as alfo in
what degree he would honour Count *Struenfee*
herewith. The ordonnance of July 14, expreffes: "That the minifter fhall write down,
and digeft, all orders which his Majefty fhall
think proper to give him verbally, and either
lay them before His Majefty, to receive his
fignature; or elfe fign them himfelf in the
King's name, and iffue them under the feal of
the cabinet; to which every one was to yield
due obedience." It was, therefore, not the
fon of the minifter, but folely the orders
which the King gave him, and ordered him
iffue, that received any authority by the aforefaid ordonnance. The cabinet was properly the
King himfelf, and Count *Struenfee* was fo far from
thinking that he could be confidered as fuch,
that in all cafes, when any one fpoke, or wrote to
him

him about ftate affairs, he always gave for anfwer, that they muft apply to the Cabinet, or to
His Majefty. The affair of lieutenant-general
Huht, and many other inftances, can prove the
truth hereof.

Nothing was tranfacted in the cabinet, nor
iffued from it, but under royal authority. The
King, who heard and examined every thing that
came to the Cabinet, either from the different
departments of ftate, or from others, gave his decifion, either in writing or verbally. Nothing could
efcape His Majefty's attention, becaufe every
thing came feveral times under his eyes; *firft*
when an order was iffued from the Cabinet; *fe-
condly*, when the report of its execution, or a remonftrance againft it, came from thofe to whom
it had been addreffed; and, *thirdly*, when the
weekly extract of all orders, &c. iffued from the
Cabinet, was laid before him for approbation.
Every thing was, and fhould be, tranfacted in His
Majefty's name. The beft proof, that fuch was
His Majefty's abfolute will and pleafure, and that
the King, after mature confideration, and from
his own accord and free will, named Count
Struenfee his Prime Minifter of the Cabinet, is
that every letter of the above-mentioned ordonnance of July 14, is in His Majefty's own hand
writing, for which I refer this Moft Honourable
Commiffion to the records (*Lit. — p. —*) — As
therefore, no room remains to fufpect the leaft
furprife in this appointment, fo nothing can be
conftrued an attempt to ufurp the royal power.
It alfo appears, indeed, that what is here laid to
the charge of Count *Struenfee*, rather confifts in
fome thing that *might have* happened, than in
what *has* happened. For the Attorney-General
principally

principally dwells upon the danger that was to be dreaded, in cafe Count *Struenfee* fhould abufe the King's confidence, and iffue orders different to thofe given him by His Majefty. To hinder this, it is faid, " the Law enjoins the King to " fign eveiy thing himfelf, and declares guilty " of High Tieafon, whoever fhall affume any " thing contrary thereto." But I hope to prove, that there is little foundation for this argument.

The Law would certainly be veiy unjuft, if it punifhed any individual, merely becaufe he had an opportunity of committing mifdemeanors, though he had never made ufe of fuch an oppor- tunity, and Count *Struenfee* can therefore not be punifhed, fince, though he had it in his power to abufe His Majefty's confidence, yet it cannot be proved, that he really made any unjuft ufe of it. The Law implies no fuch thing; for the two articles, above quoted, are not at all confonant with the point in queftion. It is true, that the Law, Art. 7, ordains: that " all bufinefs concern- " ing the ftate and government fhall be tranf- " acted in no other name than that of the King, " and under his feal; and that the King, if of " age, fhall fign every thing himfelf." It is alfo true, that in Art. 26. it is declared: " that " whoever fhall undertake or execute any thing " tending to leffen the King's powei and autho- " rity, fhall be deemed an offender againft the " Majefty of the King, and be punifhed accord- " ingly." But what is it, that Count *Struenfee* has undertaken or executed to leffen the power and authority of the King?—He cannot be charged with any tranfgreffion of the firft part of Art. 7. for no one can deny, that all ftate af- fairs have been tranfacted in the King's name, and

and under his feal. Is it then, becaufe his Majefty did not chufe to fign all orders from the
Cabinet himfelf?—In this cafe I muft beg leave
to obferve, that this part of the Article entirely
concerns His Majefty, and no other; and if the
Attorney-General means to prove in this any tranfgreffion againft the Law, and make any one accountable for it, it cannot be Count *Strvenfee.*
It always depended upon his Majefty, to fign all
orders and other affairs, if he pleafed; when,
therefore, His Majefty did not chufe to fign any
papers, but ordered Count *Strvenfee* to fign them
in his name, it is ridiculous to fuppofe, that
Count *Struenfee*'s obedience to the King's fpecial
commands, can be deemed derogatory to the
royal authority. Let us further confider, that
according to the true fenfe of the Law, the figning an order, &c. in the name and inftead of the
King, cannot be deemed an offence againft the
dignity of the crown: For, according to the 13th
Article, the King is to make oath, that he will
fuffer no infringement upon the fole fovereign
power vefted in him, which oath would be contradictory to what has been cuftomary under this
and all preceding reigns, if the fignature was an
effential part of the fole fovereign power; fince,
in many inftances, the different departments, as
well as former minifters, have made known to the
fubjects the Sovereign's will and command, without the King's fignature to fuch ordonnances.
And let us even fuppofe the very worft in this
affair; let us fuppofe that in this a fault had been
committed: His Majefty's moft gracious and abfolute command of July 14, muft be fufficient to
fcreen Count *Struenfee* from being called to an
account, becaufe he acted merely according to
the

the King's orders, and to fhew his due and moft
fubmiffive obedience to his royal mafter's will
and pleafure, and unlefs this is a fufficient protection, no fubject would be fecure in the execution of his fovereign's commands

The Attorney-General mentions, in his Memorial, Sect. 5, 6, and 7, fome inftances whereby he
means to prove, that Count *Struenfee* has actually
abufed his Majefty's confidence, and the power he
was entrufted with, by figning and iffuing orders
from the Cabinet without the King's knowledge
or inftructions. The firft of thefe is the difbanding
the body-guard, in which he even fuppofes the
Count had fome very dangerous views againft
the King or the ftate.

The true caufe of this operation was, that many perfons were of opinion, that the guard was, in
feveral refpects prejudicial to the army, as appears
from the Count's anfwers to the different queftions
upon the records (*Lit.* — *p.* —) and from the
different writings quoted by him. The Count
moft fincerely vouches, that this affair was
not as reprefented by the Attorney-General,
namely, without the previous knowledge of his
Majefty. He remembers very well, that this
has often been the fubject of converfation between
his Majefty and himfelf, and that he read to the
King the whole order of December 21, for difbanding the foot-guard, before it was iffued from
the Cabinet; alfo, that as foon as the remonftrance
came from the war-office, the King, inftead of
liftening thereto, immediately confirmed this order
in his own hand-writing. The fecond order of December 24, which properly tended to cafhiering
the faid guard, becaufe they had refufed obedience
to the firft order, was alfo figned with his Ma-

F   jefty's

jefty's own hand, before it was fent to Lieutenant-General *Gahler*. What the Attorney-General further means to intimate, by faying, that the extracts of feveral orders were kept back, with a view that the King might approve of both the aforefaid orders at the fame time, is as little founded on truth as the reft, for, befides that it would have been much eafier to furprize or deceive his Majefty by a long, formal and tedious order, than by a fhort abftract from the fame. it was not confonant with the regular courfe of bufinefs, that the extracts from the feveral orders fhould be laid before his Majefty, for approbation, before the end of the week. And, in cafe any fault had happened in this, the declarations of both Privy Secretaries *Panning* and *Moras* abfolutely fhew, that this muft have been their fault, and not Count *Struenfee*'s.

The fecond inftance mentioned by the Attorney-General, Sect. 6. relates to the different prefents and fums of money, Count *Struenfee* procured for himfelf and his friends; and particularly thofe, fince the fettling of the accounts of his Majefty's treafury, for the months of April and May, in which the Attorney-General attempts even to prove a fraud. With regard to the prefents and gratifications, it is fufficient for Count *Struenfee*'s exculpation, to fay, that his Majefty has been pleafed to give and approve of them. The Count is fully perfuaded, that whoever will examine and compare the accounts, before and fince he had the direction of the treafury, will find that fuch prefents were not unufual, and that much larger fums were before given to others. But what the Attorney-General mentions concerning the fraud, the Count perceives, with the greateft grief, that even his Majefty

jefty feems to bear witnefs againft him. But as he has, in his own Memorial, moft fincerely affured his judges, that he is not guilty of this crime, he hopes he fhall be allowed to mention every circum-ftance which can contribute to prove his innocence.

The Attorney-General makes ufe of two fuppofitions to prove this fraud. *Firft,* that " a nullo has been added to the two fums " of 6000, and that they have been changed " into 60000 rixdollars." *Secondly,* " that the " name of *Falkenfchiold,* with the fum of 2000 " rixdollars, has been inferted after the inftru-" ment had received his Majefty's approbation." That this certainly was not the cafe, the inftru-ment itfelf will prove, in which all the fi-gures of the four different fums, together with *Falkenfchiold's* name, are written with one and the fame ink, wherewith His Majefty wrote the ap-probation to thefe different fums. Not to men-tion, that his Majefty, in conformity with many former and fubfequent accounts, would have writ-ten much higher up, had not the name of *Falken-fchiold* ftood there before the royal approbation was added to it. It is true, that the total fum ap-pears to be written with different ink, and that, in this, the figure of 3 feems to have been a 2 before. But the firft is of no manner of confequence, con-fidering that the whole was not caft up till after his Majefty had approved of the different fums that were to be expreffed in this one; and the other may eafily have proceeded from an error of the pen, in cafting up; and as fuch it has been looked upon by *Panmg* and others, as appears upon the records (*Lit.* — *p.* —) But, to prove more clearly the fallacy of the Attorney-General's fuppofitions, I beg leave to obferve:

F 2

1. That

1. That Count *Struenfee* was under no neceffity to make ufe of any fuch means to obtain money, becaufe his Majefty never refufed him, whenever he folicited for any, and becaufe he had an hundred other opportunities to acquire riches, if he could have fubmitted to make ufe of any unlawful means, of which however not a fingle inftance is mentioned in the accufation.

2. Count *Strunfee* has never made a fecret of having received fuch a fum as in cafe of a fraud it may be naturally fuppofed he would; for Baron *Schimmelmann,* (who as high treafurer paid the different fums) befides many other perfons, knew of it at the time; and when Count *Brandt,* on the fame day, thanked his Majefty for his prefent, the King faid to him, " It is but juft, that I fhould " make fome provifion for you." (See the records, *Lit.* — *p.* —) from which anfwer it certainly appears that it muft have been a confiderable fum.

3. It was impoffible to keep this a fecret from his Majefty; for on fettling the accounts foon after, the different fums were mentioned again in the book, and the balance was carried over to a new account, which accounts were infpected and afterwards approved of by his Majefty; and thus the different prefents a fecond time received his approbation. (vid. *Lit.* — *p.* —)

I therefore hope, that from thefe different matters of fact, it will appear clearly, that nothing unfair has been practifed in this tranfaction; but that every thing is in reality fuch as ftated by Count *Struenfee* in his anfwers to the different queftions, (*Lit.*— *p.* —)

The third inftance, Sect. 7. relates to the fale of the diamond nofegay. But as this was intirely her Majefty's doing, and as the Count never knew otherwife than that his Majefty had confented to the fale of this jewel, he never thought that he fhould be called to an account for it. What he has done in this affair, has been in obedience to the Queen's commands; and as he has not derived the leaft advantage from it, it cannot be laid to his charge if the full value has not been paid for the jewel, which however has not yet been clearly proved.

Thefe are the chief accufations, Count *Struenfee* ftands charged with, fo far at leaft, as they concern his adminiftration. The Attorney-General touches, indeed, in feveral places of his plea, on fome other trifling circumftances, as for inftance, the appointment of the Count's brother to the head of the department of finances, &c. But as thefe were the natural confequences of the principles of adminiftration adopted by the King himfel, the execution of which hath been fealed with his moft fpecial approbation, it would be needlefs to dwell any longer upon that fubject.

I will rather fhew, before I conclude this part, that the Attorney-General accufes Count *Struenfee* without reafon, when he reprefents him as " hav-" ing had fome very bad and dangerous views " againft the King and the ftate in his admini-" ftration," and that " he hath endeavoured to " maintain himfelf, by unlawful means, in " the feveral ftations in which his Majefty had " been pleafed to place him " In order to prove the firft of thefe accufations, he particularly mentions the difbanding of the life-guard, and then the loading and keeping a certain number of can-

non

non in readiness.—What gave occasion to the first, has been circumstantially explained, and sufficiently justified in court, and the depositions of Major General *Gude*, those of Count *Struensee*, together with the confrontation, (*Lit. — p. —*) manifestly shew, that the loading of the cannon was done with no other intent than to keep the populace in awe, for the sake of public tranquility; and that Count *Struensee* never gave any positive order in that affair, but that Major General *Gude*, who then had the command of the city, thought it as unavoidably connected with the general injunction he had received, to keep every thing in readiness for the maintainance of peace and good order. Neither is it proved nor probable, that the Count hath, or would have done any thing, to secure his retreat, in case he had failed in the attempt, the Attorney-General lays to his charge in the 9th Section, of assuming the title and character of a *Protector*.—Every witness and instrument produced in court, during the course of this inquisition, clears him from the charge of high treason against the person of his Majesty; and the Attorney-General himself confesses it. And indeed, is it probable that Count *Struensee*'s gratitude or prudence could have suffered him to carry on so infamous a scheme?—It was to the King alone he owed his elevation and success; his Majesty's confidence and protection were the sole supporters of his grandeur, and the only fences for his security.—But let us suppose him even to have been wicked enough, to set aside all sense of his duty, where is then the party he must have formed to put his scheme into execution?—Is it to be supposed, that in such a case he would have been imprudent enough to acquaint the public at large with his design, as the loading of the cannon, according

cording to the Attorney-General's opinion, feems
to infinuate?—He certainly would have taken
furer meafures to fecure himfelf againft fuch accidents as might, and as actually have happened
to him; efpecially, as we fee from the depofitions of
C. Naffe and Count *Brandt*, that he had been informed of what the Attorney-General calls the
ftorm that hung over his head, long before it
burfted.

It is equally unjuft to affert that Count *Struenfee*
employed other unlawful means to maintain himfelf
in the different ftations the King had been pleafed
to place him in. To prove this, it is faid, " that
" Count *Brandt* was placed by his Majefty to
" obferve, and to keep other perfons from him,"
but whoever fhall clofely examine this charge,
will foon find its futility.—Is it poffible that a
Monarch who daily appears in a numerous affembly at court, and other public places, can remain
a ftranger to what publicly paffes in his dominions, concerning his government?—Or is it natural to fuppofe, that Count *Brandt* could hinder
the King from fpeaking to any perfon whenever
he pleafed?—And in cafe it had been fo, were
there none that could write, and are there not a
thoufand different ways and means to convey a
petition or memorial into the hands of a Sovereign, without any one, of what ftation foever,
being able to prevent it?-- Count *Brandt* was
abfent from his Majefty and the court for days
and weeks together, which certainly afforded
fufficient opportunities to lay before the King all
grievances the nation laboured under, had there
been in reality any caufe for fuch complaints.
Befides this, Count *Brandt* has afferted the contrary (*Lit.* -- *p*, —) and moreover declared, that
Count

Count *Struenſee* did not want his aſſiſtance to keep
up his credit; for no one, beſides himſelf, poſ-
ſeſſed a greater ſhare of his Majeſty's confidence.—Nor does this charge appear to be in the
leaſt ſtrengthened by what the Attorney General
mentions in the 8th Sect. of his accuſation;
namely, " That Count *Struenſee* gave orders,
" that all letters, packets and other papers direct-
" ed to the King, ſhould be delivered into the
Cabinet."—For, beſides that, in caſe there had
been any particular view in it, this order muſt
have been given long before, it was not only conformable to his Majeſty's will and pleaſure; but
it alſo appears from the depoſitions of the two
ſecretaries, *Paning* and *Merais*, as alſo from that of
Count *Struenſee* (*Lit.* — *p.* —) that it was abſolutely neceſſary for the diſpatch of buſineſs, and to
reſtore order and regularity to all letters and other
ſtate papers, which had before, in the King's
apartments, been thrown about in the greateſt confuſion; and that, after this, his Majeſty received
all letters, packets and other papers, with the ſame
regularity as before.

Thus I flatter myſelf to have ſhewn, that Count
Struenſee has done nothing without his Majeſty's
knowledge and conſent, as far as it concerns the
accuſations relative to his adminiſtration; that he
never had any view of acquiring credit and power
at the expence of the King's authority; and that,
if he has failed in ſome reſpect, it is not to be
imputed to any voluntary and premeditated deſign, which deſerves the contemptuous expreſ-
ſions the Attorney-General makes uſe of, but to
that weakneſs and imprudence, to which every
human being is liable. From this it will therefore
appear, that nothing has been proved which can

give

give the leaſt reaſon to apprehend, that Count *Struenſee* had any deſign upon the royal authority, or the leaſt idea of ill-treating his King and his benefactor. He declares, till this very moment, as he always has done, that the promotion of his Majeſty's happineſs, the fulfilling of his wiſhes to further the proſperity of the empire, ſolely and entirely directed all his views.

I proceed to the *ſecond part* of the accuſation, which relates to the injuries, ſaid to be done to the different perſons of the Royal Family.—For what concerns the coolneſs and indifference wherewith her Majeſty, the Queen Dowager *Juliana Maria,* and his Royal Highneſs Prince *Frederick,* are aſſerted to have been treated, Count *Struenſee* declares, that the true and real motive for it has been aſſigned in his examination, and appears upon the records (*Lit. — p. —*) that he never countenanced theſe meaſures;' that he knows of no other reaſon for a ſeparate box being aſſigned to the Prince at the Theatre, than that it was the King's diſlike 'to the Prince's retinue being admitted into the ſame box with his Majeſty; and that he was an entire ſtranger to the correſpondence occaſioned on that account between Count *Schulin* and Count *Brandt.*

Concerning the education of his Royal Highneſs the Hereditary Prince, I refer to Count *Struenſee*'s own Memorial, where he poſitively declares, that he never had any ſuch views as the Attorney-General lays to his charge. He is, in this reſpect, ſo ſenſible of his innocence and the purity of his intentions, that he ſcruples not to ſubmit himſelf to the deciſion of the ableſt phyſicians, whether his plan of education was not calculated to reſtore

and

and ſtrengthen, and whether it did not in reality reſtore and ſtrengthen the Prince's health and conſtitution. Beſides, it was the Queen's abſolute will
that things ſhould be ſo conducted, and he has often
incurred her Majeſty's diſpleaſure by repreſenting,
that he thought the due bounds were in ſome reſpects exceeded.

In regard to what happened between his Majeſty and Count *Brandt*, and what the Attorney-
General lays to the charge of Count *Struenſee*, in
the 2d Sect. of his Accuſation, the Count declares
now, as he has done in the examination (*Lit.* —
p. —) that he never could believe Count *Brandt*
would have taken the affair upon the ſerious foot-
ing he did; but always thought the whole
would have been accommodated between the King
and Count *Brandt*, in *a jocular manner*. His advice was, that Count *Brandt* ſhould keep himſelf
at ſome diſtance, and wait till the King ſhould
deſire and force him to make reſiſtance; but it
evidently appears that Count *Brandt* did not expect Count *Struenſee*'s previous conſent, nor ſubſe-
quent approbation; for he not only concealed from
Struenſee upon what plan he was determined
to act, ſaying only, he intended to call the King
to an account for the offence he had given
him; but alſo, after the affair had happened he
never mentioned a word concerning the moſt aggravating circumſtances, namely, the horſewhip,
the faſtening of the bolt, and his challenge and
abuſive language. What therefore concerns the
ſhare and knowledge Count *Struenſee* had of this
affair, he is the more inclined to hope that he can
juſtify himſelf, as on ſuch occaſions his Majeſty
deſired never to be treated as King, but as a private perſon; and for this reaſon only he did not
oppoſe

oppofe Count *Brandt*'s defign. His innocence in this affair alfo corroborates the proof, that he never thought of fetting afide the profound refpect due to his King, and that no one can fay he ever failed in that point.—What the Attorney-General afferts, on the ftrength of the declarations he produces of feveral witneffes, is a matter of mere converfation, void of all foundation; neither is there a better proof to be deduced from the letter he quotes, that Count *Brandt* was to be rewarded for what he did, fince that letter was written in the beginning of September, 1771, as proved by *Paning* (*Lit.* — *p.* —) and the affair between the King and *Brandt* did not happen until fome time after.

Thus, I hope, that every thing the Attorney-General has laid to the charge of Count *Struenfee*, will appear in a light very different to that in which he has placed it; and in cafe this fhould not prove fufficient for his juftification, Count *Struenfee* flies to that mercy, which his Majefty has been fo often pleafed to make him experience. He alfo throws himfelf at his Majefty's feet, moft humbly craving pardon for the crime the Attorney-General has mentioned in the firft Section of his accufation, but which I have hitherto paffed unnoticed. This is the only fault of all that have been laid to his charge, of which he knows himfelf guilty, being confcious, that in this he has offended his King and benefactor. He fears, however, and laments with grief and forrow, that his crime is too great, to hope for mercy; yet, if the confideration of the frailty of human nature, a true fenfe of his guilt, a fincere repentance, the flowing of unfeigned tears,

and

and the fervent prayers he addreſſes to Heaven for the proſperity of the King and the Royal Family,—if theſe can excite any compaſſion in the Royal boſom of his Sovereign, whoſe bounty, humanity and benevolence will ever remain unparalelled,—he hopes he ſhall not be thought wholly undeſerving thereof.

In all other reſpects, he is fully convinced, that the Law and his innocence will protect him, and that on theſe conſiderations he may hope for mercy and his acquittal. But, as his ſole refuge is in the clemency of his Sovereign, he begs likewiſe, that this Moſt Honourable Court, which has been a witneſs to his ſincerity, repentance and grief, will be pleaſed to make ſuch a favourable report to his Majeſty, as may tend, as much as poſſible, to the alleviation of his fate.

12 JY 62

Copenhagen,
April 22, 1772.

N. Uhldal.

T H E

THE

DEFENCE

O F

COUNT JOHN FRED. STRUENSEE,

Written by himfelf and laid before the

ROYAL COMMISSION of INQUISITION,

At COPENHAGEN.

TRANSLATED from the GERMAN ORIGINAL.

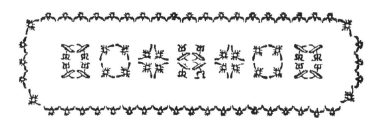

T H E

DEFENCE, &c.

IT is very difficult, and perhaps impoffible, to give a clear and exact account, and to afiert the true reafons of the feveral motives and views, which have either directed or produced every individual tranfaction or event in fuch a fituation as mine was at court. This tafk has, however, been impofed upon me, and I have anfwered the different queftions, put to me by the Royal Commiffion, as well as the nature of things would permit. But, as it is impoffible to fuppofe, that no obfcurity, error, or apparent contradictions, fhould have crept into my account, I will therefore endeavour to make fome amends for thefe defects, by a true narrative of the motives and circumftances that have given occafion to the tranfactions I have either been partly concerned in, or the fole caufe of; and I fhall be the more fincere, as I am quite
uninfluenced

uninfluenced by the thought, whether such a narrative will tend to exculpate me, or to aggravate my guilt   To do this the more effectually, I shall first shew, by what means I have gained that interest, to which I owe my former prosperity, how I conducted myself when possessed thereof, and to what purposes I have made it instrumental.

I must confess, that an indefatigable activity, added to the particular care I took to make use of even the smallest opportunities and advantages, which either offered themselves, or were improved by my endeavours, have contributed more to my elevation and success, than mere chance or accidents.   Riches and honours were not, however, what I chiefly aimed at; at least I only looked upon them as a very uncertain and distant consequence of my endeavours. I had chosen but one way to obtain them, and I was fully determined, rather to give up all views of that kind, than employ any unlawful means to accomplish them.   An ardent desire of rendering myself useful, by actions that could be of real and extensive benefit to the society I lived in, was the only object of my wishes.   My residence at Altona afforded me some hopes of satisfying that desire, and my friends, amongst whom the two Counts *Rantzau Aschberg*, the Count *Brandt*, and Count *Holck*, were the most active, at last succeeded to place me upon a more spacious and conspicuous stage.   Though some of these friends thought they discovered in me abilities fit for more extensive undertakings than the practice of physic; yet my inclinations were so attached to my profession, that I should entirely have devoted myself to it, had not more flattering objects diverted my attention.

attention. This inclination followed me to court, and I found it the more neceſſary to indulge it, as I was ſuſpected by all, who were not prejudiced in my favour. During his Majeſty's journey abroad, I was attentive to nothing but what concerned his health; and, as the King gave me frequent opportunities to be with him, I endeavoured, as much as lay in my power, to render my attendance uſeful and agreeable, by reading and converſation. Politics were entirely baniſhed, or if now and then admitted, they were kept within general bounds, and without the leaſt reflection upon the ſituation of affairs at that time, to which I was then an intire ſtranger. I contented myſelf with what I ſaw, and always avoided to receive any information on that ſubject, either from the King himſelf or any one elſe. My correſpondence with my friends was broken off, or was upon indifferent ſubjects. His Majeſty's perſon was the only object of my care and attention; and it was for that reaſon, that I more than once quarrelled with Count *Holck*, and oppoſed him in things I thought wrong and detrimental to his Majeſty's conſtitution.

The only point I had then in view, was that I endeavoured to leſſen that extenſive power Count *Holck* had acquired over the King, by adviſing his Majeſty to conſider and examine every thing himſelf, and not blindly to follow the advice of any one. My intention was by no means to injure the Count in the opinion of his Majeſty, tho' a favourable opportunity for that purpoſe preſented itſelf at Paris, when Count *Holck* had much incurred the King's diſpleaſure; and when Count *Brandt* (who was come to Paris unknown to me) with many other perſons and circumſtances,

would

would have contributed to leffen his credit. It is eafy to conceive, how little this conduct was calculated to make my fortune; neither did I ever take any advantage of the favourable opportunities I more than once met with during the journey, to afk or obtain any thing, either for myfelf or my friends; and it was owing entirely to the care of Count *Bernftorff* and Baron *Schimmelmann,* that I accompanied the King to Copenhagen, with a falary of 1000 rixdollars *per ann.* and received a gratification of 500 rixdollars for the journey in 1769.

My conduct, and the objects of my attention, were for the firft fix months after his Majefty's return, the fame as during the journey. I had entirely devoted myfelf to the care of his perfon, and took no concern in any matters, but fuch as related immediately thereto. It was to that object alone I directed and applied all the influence the King's confidence had given me over him, and I ftudied to excite in him a defire for application and exercife, and to bring him to a regular and well-planned way of living. This defign induced me never to foibear mentioning to his Majefty, without the leaft referve or difguife, what I thought was proper for him, not fuffering myfelf to be with-held by the fear of lofing his favours; though I frequently obferved, that I was received with coolnefs, which happened the oftener, as thofe who feeked to ingratiate themfelves with his Majefty, did not remain inactive on fuch occafions. His Majefty will eafily recollect how often this has happened, efpecially when I have reprefented to him, the dreadful effects of a premature, inconfiderate, and unbounded gratification of the *fenfual appetites*; when I have endeavoured to pre

'vent him from trying painful, pernicious, and unneceffary experiments upon himfelf, and ftrove
to recall him from falfe, unjuft, and dangerous
notions and defigns.

The only connection I had at that time at
court, and that had any influence upon his Majefty, was with Count *Holck* and the Chamberlain *von Warnftedt*. The former of thefe ufed
much referve; but the other honoured me now
and then with his confidence, which gave me an
opportunity of communicating fuch principles
and ideas, as I knew would be of fervice to his
Majefty, if properly fuggefted to him, and which
the Chamberlain had many opportunities to do.
When afterwards the court fpent the fummer
feafon at *Friedrickfburg*, I made feveral new ac-
quaintances, and towards the end of the feafon, I
was concerned in feveral things that happened,
and thereby difcovered the different views of the
then courtiers. The court was at that time di-
vided into three parties, *viz.* that of Count
Holck, that of Count *Fritz von Moltke*, and that
of Lady *Gahler*. The firft was fupported by the
favour Count *Holck* poffeffed, and by his connection with the different minifters of ftate, or
rather their indifference to hurt him. The fecond
ftudied to find a fupport in the Queen, relied upon the protection of the Ruffian Ambaffadour,
and was defirous of having either the Chamberlain *Warnftedt*, or me, on their fide. The third
can hardly be called a party, as it confifted only
of Lady *Gähler*, who ftudied to employ the influence fhe endeavoured to gain over the King,
to awaken him out of that ftate of indolence and
inactivity, in which fhe thought him involved.
The two laft aimed, as we may eafily conceive, at

the

the difmiffion of Count *Holck*. I muft needs fay, that my ideas and inclinations coincided beft with Lady *Gahler*'s views, whofe intentions I thought fair and juft. In two points, however, I could not entirely agree with her. The *firft* was, that fhe wifhed, at any rate, to remove Count *Holck*, which I thought unneceffary: as it was not difficult to infpire the King with better and more conftant principles, it was natural that the Count's credit, which was already upon the decline, would foon lofe all its weight, and that in general a new favourite was more to be dreaded than an old one, whofe views and inclinations are once known. The *fecond* point we differed in, was, that fhe would not enter into my notions, that the fole and beft method to make the King really and truly happy, was to leffen his diflike for the Queen, and to eftablifh a real and reciprocal confidence between them. Lady *Gahler* thought herfelf affronted and injured by the Queen, and feemed refolved not to feek her favours, till after fhe fhould have it in her power, to be ufeful to her Majefty, through the influence gained over the King. I endeavoured to convince Count *Moltke*'s party (as far as they placed any confidence in me) how little hopes they had of ruining Count *Holck*, and to how many difagreeable circumftances the Queen would be expofed, if fhe was to exert any authority, that was not founded upon the King's confidence and approbation.

Towards the latter end of the fummer, 1769, I had frequent opportunities of converfing with the Queen, and her Majefty was gracioufly pleafed to entruft me with her ideas concerning her fituation, with which I found fhe was extremely difpleafed, had no hopes of ever living

happy

happy with the King, or to have any fatisfaction
and peace, in the then prefent circumftances.
Thefe notions were ftrengthened and confirmed
by the continual advices her Majefty received of
every thing difagreeable that paffed at court.
The object of her difpleafure was, however, not
the King, but Count *Holck*, whom fhe looked
upon as the author of all the misfortunes fhe had
experienced, and was ftill threatened with She
did not fo much mind the ill treatment fhe received from the King himfelf, and endeavoured
only to fecure herfelf againft them by folitude
and indifference, which however ferved to increafe
their mutual coolnefs and diflike. My fituation
in thefe circumftances was very perplexed and
critical. On one fide, the Queen made me the
confidant of her diffatisfaction, and on the other,
I was a conftant witnefs of the King's difcontent,
vexation, and his defire to extricate himfelf from all
that was difagreeable to him. I was to give advice to both, and thought myfelf in duty bound
to ufe my utmoft efforts to operate their reconci-
liation. I acted on this principle, that their happinefs folely depended upon their union, though
I had but little hopes of fuccefs. I endeavoured
to perfuade the Queen, that the true and only
way to render her fituation agreeable, was for her
to ftrive to gain his Majefty's confidence, and that
this could not be done by any other means than by
complaifance, by condefcending to his will, an-
ticipating his wifhes, and endeavouring to render
her company, in every refpect, as agreeable as
poffible. I begg'd her Majefty would be pleafed
never to liften to any infinuations whatever againft
the King, but to obferve and examine every thing
herfelf. I endeavoured even to diminifh or fup-

prefs

prefs her diflike for Count *Holck*, and the Count,
on his part, did all he could to make himfelf
agreeable to her Majefty; but his efforts generally produced a contrary effect, and the diflike
againft him was fo ftrong, that nothing could
over-power it. On the other hand, I endeavoured to engage the King to be polite towards
the Queen, without being fo formal and cere-
monious as he had ufed to be with her, fince
his return from abroad, which was not only unneceffary, but often degenerated into an ironical
condefcenfion, much more difpleafing to her
Majefty, than a real want of due attention, and
which of courfe broke off all confidence between them. Their Majefties perfectly agreed
in one thing, which contributed much to promote the union they afterwards lived in : I mean
that they were both heartily tired of their un-
eafy fituation, and even often wifhed to be dif-
incumbered of their rank and dignity.

Count *Holck* had, long before the King's journey to Holftein, in 1770, loft much of his influence, and was fupported only by the credit of
his relations, and becaufe no one thought it
prudent to wrong him before his Majefty. He
gave the finifhing ftroke to his own intereft,
when he placed young Baron *Hauch* by the King
as page of the back ftairs, in order to fupplant
Baron *Warnftedt*, who from that time increafed
in favour. The Count propofed that journey
with a view, as I believe, to reinftate himfelf
into the King's grace; but that very journey
proved his deftruction. The Queen ftill per-
fifted in the fame notions, that no peace and
quietnefs were to be expected at court, fo long
as the Count remained there; though I ftrove,

to perfuade her, that it was by no means advantageous, and becoming the King's chaiacter, that the greateft favourites and confidants fhould be difcarded at the firft opportunity, and that it was infinitely bettei for his Majefty to know them thoioughly, and examine their private views himfelf, which was the beft method of guaiding againft favourites. I repiefented, moreover, the Count as lefs dangerous, fince he had loft all his influence. But all my perfuafions were to no purpofe; and to fet hei Majefty at laft at eafe, I propofed to place Count *Brandt* at couit, and to call Lieut. General Count *Rantzau Afcheberg* to Copenhagen. They both were peifonally very agreeable to the King, and the latter very fit to counterbalance the authority of the miniftry, which the Queen feared, would endeavour to reftore Count *Holck* into favour, by removing thofe that were againft him.

The only motive of thefe meafures was to reftore peace and fecurity at court, without the leaft view or plan of the different changes in the adminiftration which have happened fince; for the Queen had not the leaft inclination to interfere in ftate affairs.—Count *Brandt* came accordingly to court at Schleffwig, and Count *Rantzau* at Traventhal. Count *Holck* quitted the court by the King's orders, yet I cannot help obferving, that thofe who were about his Majefty, contributed much to it. From that time feveral other things happened at court, and fome alterations took place, the fprings and fecret motions of which I fhall foon expofe to view. I muft, however, previoufly obferve, that all the intereft I had at that time, confifted

merely

merely in the perfonal confidence his Majefty
was pleafed to place in me; that I never employed my influence but in fuch cafes as concerned immediately and directly the King's
perfon; and that my profperity and circumftances of life were as follow: I was Counfellor of
Conference, and reader to his Majefty, with a
falary of 1500 rixdollars *per ann.* I had debts
to the amount of nearly 5000 rixdollars, which
I had partly contracted at Altona, but the greateft part during the journey abroad, and had
never received an extraordinary prefent from the
King, except the 500 rixdollars already mentioned, and a horfe. I never afked any thing,
either for myfelf or my friends, unlefs I here
admit my having been inftrumental in Count
Brandt's receiving an addition of 400 rixdollars
to his falary, and that his Majefty has twice prefented Count *Holck* with the fum of 10,000
rixdollars each time. Thus were matters cir-
cumftanced, before any changes in the miniftry
took place,

    I cannot deny, that though I had no per-
fonal objection againft any of the minifters, I
was rather prejudiced againft their meafures,
than an admirer of their adminiftration. I had
ftrongly imbibed this notion long before I came
to court; nor had I any reafon to change my
opinion, or doubt the veracity of thofe, from
whofe informations I had formed my ideas,
fince I was fully confirmed in every thing, by
what I afterwards heard and faw in Copenhagen.
The following are the principal objections,
that were generally made againft the adminiftration of that time.

1, That

1. That it was a maxim eftablifhed by cuftom, to divert the King from all ftate affairs, by infpiring him with a diflike to them, in multiplying his mechanical occupations, and rendering government a heavy and difficult tafk for him. Matters were never fuggefted to him, but in obfcure and prolix phrafes, or long fpeeches and declamations, crowded with unneceffary detail; that he was feldom allowed a free decifion between two opinions, but was in fome meafure forced to decide in favour of that the miniftry had previoufly adopted; and that they generally endeavoured to engage his attention to accidental trifles, in order that matters of confequence might make lefs impreffion upon him (*).

2. That the King had fo little authority, that he had no will of his own in the moft minute things, not even in the conduct of his private life; fo that thofe who were attached to him, who had acquired his confidence, and ftudied to pleafe his inclination, were fure to be undone; whilft others, who oppofed his tafte, were encouraged and fupported.

3. That favours and intrigues had too great an influence upon all tranfactions; that the moft important dignities and places were given to courtiers, whofe only merit confifted in having

ing

(*) What *Struenfee* here advances, with refpect to the Danifh adminiftration, may undoubtedly, with equal juftice and propriety, be applied to fome other courts in Europe; where adminiftration, with a view to keep their Sovereign from enquiring *too nicely* into their conduct, infpire him with a tafte for thofe *mechanical* employments, which are proper only for the laborious part of his fubjects.

ing lived a few years at court in the capacity of page, or gentleman of the bed-chamber, &c. and that all the other places were given to creatures or servants of thofe perfons and families, who maintained each other in the poffeffion of credit and authority.

4. That an univerfal anarchy had taken place; that none would, nor dared to make ufe of his authority, for fear of ruining himfelf; that every one endeavoured to foar above his fphere, and to acquire influence over others; that fubordination was no where to be met with; that the occupations of the chiefs, in the different departments, confifted principally in confultations, giving advice, making enquiries, finding out modifications and expedients in matters that did not concern them; and that the inferior officers, inftead of paying due and implicit obedience to an order, only endeavoured to evade it, by finding out difficulties, and making objections and remonftrances againft it.

5. That the finances were exhaufted, not fo much by the difburfements of the King (though amongft them many were needlefs) but by other expenfive undertakings, as for inftance, the eftablifhment of the colonies, and expenfive manufactories; the forced encouragement given to the arts, tafte and luxury; the augmentation of the army; the fupport of a commerce ill calculated to the nature and fituation of the country, and detrimental to true and natural induftry; and particularly, by the confufion that reigned throughout this department, by the ill-planned operations,

operations, and various manœuvers, that were made ufe of to ferve private views.

6. That the influence of foreign courts and their minifters, had, for a long time, been greatly detrimental, mere complaifance having been confidered as the main fpring of all nego-ciations: hence a dependency had derived, which no advantage in the world could com-penfate; and that, in general, more money was expended, and more attention given to that part of ftate bufinefs, than the nature and fituation of the empire required.

7. That in proportion to the extent of the em-pire, there were by far too many places, di-ftinctions, and dignities, with great falaries annexed to them, and too many honorary characters: the former of thefe proved op-preffive to the nation, becaufe every one en-deavoured to live, and to enrich himfelf at the King's expence; the latter were ufelefs, and tended only to increafe pride and indo-lence. The nobility fhewed not the leaft in-clination or zeal to ferve their King with their wealth and power; nor did the lower clafs feem defirous to maintain themfelves by their own laudable induftry.

I will not take upon me to decide, how far thefe objections were well-grounded: but, for my part, I have, by experience, been fully con-vinced of the truth of them, without accufing, as the authors of thefe evils, any of the mini-fters in particular. In ftate affairs, time and confequences commonly determine the wifdom of an adminiftration; and, in the inftance be-fore us, time had produced nothing to its repu-tation

tation or honour. When, through the confidence the King had placed in me, I acquired some influence in administration, my views were to encourage his Majesty to examine every thing himself; but as this was contrary to the plan of the ministry, I thought it necessary the King should have persons about him, who differed in opinion from his ministers. The several resolutions and changes, which successively took place soon after, originated more from his Majesty's own will and disposition, and from accidental circumstances, than from any design, or fixed plan, at least traced by me. No persuasion or incitement were necessary, for his Majesty was more than willing to make these changes, and it is well known, that even from his ascension to the throne, he was desirous of a change in the administration. As soon as I was admitted to the King's confidence, I found his mind deeply impressed against the ministry, and it hath continued so ever since. It is true that, as far as I thought these impressions just, I never endeavoured to check them; but it is also true, that before the journey to Holstein took place, I never gave the King any favourable idea of the persons in the opposite party. For, besides the above-mentioned general objections against the administration, which had made more or less impression upon his Majesty's mind, he had several others, which concerned him personally; as for instance:

1. He was sensible, that the ministers assumed all real authority, and were looked upon as the chiefs, whom every one must endeavour to please, and on whom every thing in government

vernment depended; they left him nothing
but an empty title, and the burthen of reprefentation; and whenever they did him the
honour to require his confent or authority, it
was only to cover their faults, or to give a
fanction to their intrigues.

2. The affairs of Denmark were in fuch a ftate
of confufion and ruin, and the want of money fo great, that nothing good and prof-
perous could be expected in length of time.

3. He had more than once obferved, by his own
experience, that the power and influence of
the foreign minifters were too great, and detrimental to his intereft.

4. The negociation of Holftein, in the manner
it was conducted, was too expenfive and bur-
thenfome. Several opportunities had on this
occafion been watched, and made ufe of, to
divert the King from certain refolutions, in
order to conduct the whole affair according
to their own fancy.

5. The King difliked nothing more, than to be
obliged to attend the council twice a week;
and I believe the reafon of this was, becaufe
he had, in his youth, been infpired with a certain refpect and fear for this affembly, which,
through length of time, was become habitual.
As therefore, in fuch a difpofition, and with
the impreffions he had fince received, he
could not place a real confidence in this
council, we may eafily account for the caufe
of his diflike, and the fubfequent diffolution thereof. The King often ufed to fay:
" When I am in council, and differ in
" opinion with them, I immediately per-
" ceive a difpleafure in all countenances; long
" fpeeches,

" fpeeches, folemn proteftations, and pompous
" remonftrances then enfue, and I am obliged
" to keep filent, and let them have their own
" way."

6. Some motions had been made in council, to
re-eftablifh the finances by faving, and the
minifters feemed inclined to begin with the
King's private expences, fuch as the theatre,
hunting, &c. &c. but his Majefty was of opinion, that a reformation of the finances
fhould begin upon other objects.

7. Laftly, the bad fuccefs of the expedition
againft Algiers, to which he had in fome meafure been forced to confent, grieved and vex-
ed him very much.

In fuch difpofitions was the King on his return from Holftein, and it is eafily imagined,
that he liftened the moft to thofe who were of
the fame opinion, and that thefe did not think
of infpiring him with other ideas. All attention was engaged to fee what effects and fteps
the prefence of Count *Rantzau* would produce.
He was obnoxious to the council, and Count
Bernftorf had delivered a Memorial to the King
at Traventhal, on that account, which Count
Rantzau had anfwered, affuring, at the fame
time, that he neither would be concerned in the
Holftein negociation, nor oppofe it. Unfor-
tunately, Count *Bernftorf* had introduced fome
very fevere reflections on the oppofers of the
alliance with Ruffia. This occafioned his difmiffion, and the feveral important changes in
the miniftry that followed foon after. I do not
recollect that any particular fteps were taken to
promote the fame; neither can I affert, what
influence

influence the conferences with thofe who approved of them, and particularly Count *Rantzau*, had upon His Majefty; for I have already obferved, that the King was more than willing to make thefe changes, and only waited for a favourable opportunity. All I know is, that at that time I read to the King feveral letters and memorials, concerning the fituation of affairs in general; that I received many infinuations, encouragements, and approbations, of which I afterwards made fuch ufe as I thought moft proper; that no one's advice, concerning thefe alterations, was formally afked; but that the King himfelf, in my prefence, planned the whole arrangement for thefe changes. The King, at that time, did every thing himfelf, and wrote it with his own hand. Sometimes I drew up the heads of orders or letters, which the King either followed or altered as he pleafed; but moftly compofed them himfelf, and revifed the fair copies before they were iffued from the cabinet. All letters written with his own hand, were fealed by me, in his prefence, in the cabinet.— Every one was now in hopes, that things would turn out for the better. The King attended to bufinefs with pleafure, he read and clofely examined every thing concerning the affairs of ftate, and decided upon them according to his beft conviction. In order to preferve and encourage that difpofition in him, and to adapt, as much as poffible, his occupations to his tafte, the following general plan was laid down for the management of ftate affairs, and I have always ftudied, on my part, to act agreeably to them, as much as laid in my power.

I. Con-

I. Concerning his Majesty's own affairs and occupations.

1. The King referved folely to himfelf the final decifion in all affairs whatfoever concerning his government.

2. All propofitions, addreffes, reports, &c. were to be in writing, and the King's anfwer to be given in the like manner.

3. Thefe propofitions, &c. were to be drawn up concifely and clearly, and to contain nothing but the effential points of what they related to; and that, moreover, an extract fhould be fubjoined to each, wherein the particular cafes, on which his Majefty's decifion was defired, fhould be concifely expreffed.

4. In fuch cafes, where his Majefty fhould think proper to take advice, he would either expect the opinion of the board to which the bufinefs belonged, or name a fpecial committee; yet, notwithftanding, every thing fhould be tranfacted in its refpective department.

5. The different departments fhould, as much as the nature of things would permit, be uniform in their mode of tranfacting bufinefs.

6. As the King could not himfelf direct in what manner every clafs of ftate-bufinefs fhould be executed, but expected that care from the chiefs of the different departments; fo they were to act in conformity thereto, direct their fubalterns, and make them refponfible for the faithful difcharge of their duty.

7. Every thing fhould be decided and conducted according to the Law, and upon fixed principles.

8. Finally,

8. Finally, the bufinefs of each department
fhould be diftinct from that of the other, fo
that each of them might alone tranfact and adhere to the affairs that came under its cognizance, and have no influence upon the other,
but through the King, their number fhould
alfo be diminifhed, and one board of commif-
fioners be at the head of each department.

II. Concerning foreign affairs, the King was
pleafed to eftablifh the following maxims.
1. That his Majefty defired no greater influence
over foreign Courts, than what the fituation
of his dominions and its commerce required.
2. That all expences, occafioned by the often-
tation of feveral of his Majefty's minifters
at foreign courts, fhould be faved, and thefe
minifters fhould not be allowed any influence
upon government affairs at home.
3. That the King would faithfully adhere to
the alliance with Ruffia; but, at the fame
time, expected the court of Peterfburg would
not feek any fecurity in accidental circumftances, but rely in this upon the fincerity and
uprightnefs of his Majefty's conduct, of
which the King had given the Emprefs feveral convincing proofs.
4. That no more money fhould be expended upon
the affair with Sweden than was ftipulated by
Treaty, and that his Majefty would take no cognizance of any private difputes of that court.
The King heard and read himfelf all what
could be faid for and againft the two laft articles,
and determined accordingly; whereas he never
before had any fixed idea or thorough knowledge of thefe affairs.

H   III. Con-

III. Concerning the finances, it was refolved :

1. That all bufinefs relating to the finances, fhould henceforth be referred to, and tranf-acted by one chief department only.

2. That as good order and œconomy are the on-ly means to re-eftablifh the finances, all other plans and projects, that were not founded upon thefe principles, fhould be rejected.

3. That all taxes and revenues of the crown, of what nature foever, fhould be paid into the general treafury, and all payments affigned from thence to the other departments, in or-der that his Majefty might the more eafily afcertain the ftate of his finances.

4. That all taxes fhould be fimple, in order to avoid all perplexity in the payment and col-lecting of them.

5. That all ufual contributions of natural pro-ducts, be forthwith received in a moderate equivalent in money, in order more effectually to encourage the induftry of the hufbandman, and to prevent the many abufes generally at-tending the collecting of fuch natural pro-ducts.

6. That an account of all the expences requifite for the maintenance of his Majefty and the Royal Family, be kept fepaiate from the other expences of the ftate.

7. That fuch manufactories as are not confo-nant with the nature and fituation of the kingdom, fhould not henceforth be maintained at the King's expence ; and that the encou-ragement given in future to arts, manufactures, and commerce, fhould confift in piemiums, proportioned to the utility of the object.

8. That

8. That the farming out the King's demefnes, and the natural productions of the crown lands, was preferable to the adminiftration thereof.

9. That each branch of expence fhould be properly afcertained; that each board fhould deliver an eftimate of the expences requifite in its department; and that thefe fhould not be exceeded in the courfe of the year, and,

10. That all penfions, which in general are unproportioned to the King's revenue, fhould fuffer a certain reduction.

Whoever has been acquainted with the true ftate of the finances at that time, will willingly confefs the neceffity of the feveral reformations, reductions, and alterations, that have been, or were intended to be made, in that department.

IV. In regard to the adminiftration of juftice, his Majefty was pleafed to prefcribe the following mode:

1. The King would not finally decide any caufe whatever, unlefs it had been properly and regularly difcuffed before that court of juftice, under whofe cognizance it fell, and before that court had given its opinion thereupon.

2. That the number of the courts of juftice fhould be reduced, and each be appropriated to its particular purpofe; that a certain term be fixed, in which all law-fuits fhould be finally decided; and that, in regard to juftice, every one fhould be deemed a citizen, excluding all titles, dignities, and prerogatives whatever; and,

3. That the Judges fhould have their fixed falary, and not be allowed any fees, perquifites, &c.

H 2　　　　　　V, For

V. For what concerns the military establishment of his Majesty's land-forces, I refer to
the general plan that was found among my papers,
and which appears upon the records before the
Royal Committee.

VI. With regard to the navy, his Majesty
had adopted the following maxims.

1. That the strength of the navy should not be
supposed to consist in the great number of
ships; but that those in commission should always be kept in good order, well manned and
equipped.

2. That it is highly important and necessary, to
provide a compleat store of such ammunition
as is requisite for a bombardment; and that
such, and a profusion of all other ammunition
and necessaries for the marine establishment,
be kept in constant readiness and good order.

VII. The following were the regulations
concerning the court.

1. That all superfluous expences, tending merely to ostentation, should be saved, and such
only allowed as conduced to becoming pleasure, and to support the dignity of the
crown.

2. That all amusements at court, and the company who partook of them, should be directed, and selected according to their Majesty's
pleasure and taste, without any regard to accidental considerations.

Besides all these regulations adopted by his
Majesty, I had planned several other maxims,
which I often repeated to the King, and studied

to make him fenfible of. As fome of them
may tend to elucidate feveral circumftances laid
to my charge, I beg leave to mention them
here.

1. That it is prejudicial to the intereft of the
   ftate, to feek the happinefs of the court in the
   great concourfe of perfons; for, this encou-
   rages luxury, ruins individuals, impoverifhes
   the provinces, and the lofs fuftained thereby,
   muft at laft inevitably fall on the crown.
2. That it is better that fuch of the nobility as
   have no concern, or do not chufe to be employed in ftate affairs, fhould live in the
   country on their own eftates; and that thofe
   who aimed at preferment, fhould qualify
   themfelves in the lower employments, be
   raifed gradually, and according to their merit. No exception from this rule fhould be
   made, unlefs for very material reafons; but
   not to beftow favours, or to compenfate the
   refidence of a few years at court.
3. That on the difpofal of any places under the
   government, the King fhould always give the
   preference to thofe, who were for that purpofe prefented by the board of that department, in which the vacancy had happened,
   without attending to petitions or recom-
   mendations of courtiers, or private individuals.
4. That the King fhould not grant any furvi-
   vorfhip of offices, promife of places, mono-
   polies, or other exclufive privileges, that
   might in the leaft tend to injure public or
   private intereft and property.

H 3   5. That

5. That no characters, or honorary titles, should be conferred on persons, except those annexed to the office to which they were appointed.

6. That no pensions should be granted, except in extraordinary cases, and for well-merited and essential services. Nor should any alms be distributed at court; but, instead thereof, public charities and poor families be more effectually assisted.

7. That it should not be attempted to render Copenhagen great and wealthy, by encouraging luxury, and increasing the number of consumers, to the detriment of the provinces; but that the only means to obtain this end, are the encouragement of true industry, and the promotion of trade with foreign countries. Rich people must be drawn thither by a free and agreeable manner of living.

8. That the morals of a people cannot be meliorated by civil laws, as that would be inconsistent with the freedom of mankind; but that the moral actions of men, as far as they have no influence upon public peace and security, should be subject only to the reprehension of moralists and the ministers of the gospel: because secret vices, occasioned by constraint, are often the most injurious, and always productive of hypocrisy.

These principles in general may lead the world to judge how far it has been advantageous or detrimental to his Majesty's interest, to favour me with his confidence. I allow, that after the dissolution of the Privy-Council,

affairs

affairs were not tranfacted in due form; but this was juft what thofe, who gave advice at that time, particulaily defired. Some thought it would better fhew the King's authority, and give it an air of vigilance, if much bufinefs was tianfacted in the Cabinet, and if now and then orders were iffued and executed without acquainting the different departments thereof; others, and particularly Lieut. General *Gahler*, were of the conttary opinion, and difapproved of this method. The King was pleafed with the firft, but I could not help fiding with the latter, and therefore endeavoured to fix his Majefty's attention particularly to the regulation of the departments. Neither could I approve of the propofal made by Count *Rantzau*, that all affairs fhould be prepared by feparate perfons, be prefented to the Cabinet, and (if approved of) iffued from thence, without naming the author. This gave occafion that innumerable projects, memorials, and propofals were continually fent to the Cabinet, and many infinuations were made with the King in fupport of them. I endeavouied, as much as laid in my power, to fupprefs this mode of tranfacting bufinefs, and took care, that no other orders weie iffued fiom the Cabinet, but what ielated to the foim of the departments, or to eftablifh certain general iules. In fome inftances, I could not help making exceptions from my plan; but whenever this happened, it was either to pleafe the King's fancy, or (as I willingly confefs) to afcertain the authoiity of the Cabinet. Such were, foi inftance, the inftructions for Baion *Guldenkrone*, and the expedition of Col. *Falkenfchiold*, of which no one knew any thing,

before

before it was refolved on in the Cabinet, except
a general converfation I had with the latter,
concerning this affair. The many orders, refolutions, &c. that came afterwards from the
Cabinet, moftly originated from the regular
courfe of bufinefs, from the many propofitions
and remonftrances of the different departments,
or they related to matters, concerning which
advice had been afked in the Cabinet.

My views were particularly directed to have
all the affairs of the Cabinet tranfacted in due
form, according to certain eftablifhed rules, and
to leffen them, by rejecting every thing that was
not of fufficient importance for his Majefty's
immediate confideration. Therefore I wifhed,
that no one might have any further influence
upon the Cabinet, than what his office and dignity entitled him to, and that all propofitions
fhould be firft laid before, and be confidered by
the board of that department to which the affair belonged, and if found of any utility,
from thence be fent to the Cabinet; or if the
author did not chufe that way, it might be done
in a direct memorial to the King. I eafily conceived, that it would have been productive of
much confufion, if I had liftened to all projects
and infinuations, and attempted to lay them before the King, and to carry them into execution
through the Cabinet. This induced me to be
careful not to fpeak with any one on other affairs, than what immediately related to his
office or department, and I never took notice,
but of thofe that had come to the Cabinet in
the regular way and common courfe of bufinefs.
This conduct, however advantageous it might
be for the management of affairs, proved perfonally

fonally prejudicial to me; for it drew upon me
a fufpicion, that I was diffident and diftruftful,
and that I would take no advice. Several perfons were afterwards fufpected to have great influence with me; but I moft fincerely affure,
that no perfon ever had fuch afcendancy over
me. Count *Brandt* was the only man, in whom
I put an unlimitted confidence; yet, even with
him, during the laft fix months, I fpoke but
very little concerning the affairs of ftate. In
public affairs I had no fecrets that concerned
me perfonally, and with the others I could not,
nor would not intruft any one, except Count
Brandt.

When in the year 1771, I became more materially concerned in the government of the empire, my particular defire was always, that in
public affairs, no one might look upon my perfon, but act and judge of every thing according
to his own conviction, and the nature of the
matter in queftion. For this reafon I thought
it neceffary for the King formally to declare,
that his Majefty had intrufted me with the management of the affairs of ftate in the Cabinet,
in order that it might not have the appearance
of a felf-appropriation thereof on my fide, nor
that of complaifance or favour from the different
departments and perfons, who received the neceffary orders, and were concerned in the execution of them. This occafioned his Majefty's
order from the Cabinet, of July 15, 1771,
which is fo much urged againft me, and is faid
to be againft the fundamental Laws of the empire. I moft folemnly declare, that I never
had any fuch views in this affair, as are laid to
my charge; but that my intentions were pure,

and

and totally uninfluenced by the thought of
usurping the Royal authority. As a further
proof of the truth of this, I will here mention,
with the utmost sincerity, (*) the different motives and principles from which the said order
originated, and to what purposes I have made
it instrumental.

1. I cannot deny, that according to the before-
   mentioned form and general plan for the
   management of state affairs, I have endeavoured to concentrate the Royal authority in
   the Cabinet, because I thought it necessary
   that from thence alone all positive orders, resolutions, &c. should be issued.

2. I had often observed, that Royal orders
   had been published by former ministers, or
   other persons, who had the honour of approaching his Majesty, without having any
   other foundation or authority for such proceeding, than that they had cursorily mentioned the matter to the King. This
   had often been done to serve private views,
   and might have been productive of much abuse
   and confusion, which I endeavoured to prevent, by keeping a circumstantial account,
                                              and

(*) As *Struenfee*'s assuming the Royal authority is a crime
so strongly urged against him, his denying this fact here,
in so solemn a manner, may perhaps induce some readers
to doubt the sincerity of a man who was pleading for his
life; we therefore refer to the Narrative of his Conversion,
published some time since, and particularly to the 22d and
23d conference with Dr. *Munter*, in which Count *Struenfee*
speaks much, concerning the confession he made before his
judges, and also of the defence he meant to make, and
whoever shall duly confider the situation of his mind at
that time, will have little room to question his since it.

and exact register in the Cabinet, of all orders that were from thence issued. Those persons, who had the execution of such orders, were by these means screened from all danger, and the King knew whom to make responsible, either for issuing the same, or for neglecting to yield due obedience thereto.

3. Instead that such orders formerly were perhaps never read to the King before they were made public, they now came twice, three or four times under his eyes, and it was impossible that with the slightest attention, his Majesty could remain ignorant of the least thing that was transacted in the Cabinet.

4. The King authenticated all orders by his own signature, if not upon the original that was sent to the boards of the department, at least always upon the extract that remained in the Cabinet, and upon the remonstrances or reports from the departments, who notified their reception.

5. No department could have any influence upon the other, except through the King, and proper notice thereof was always given to, and remained in the Cabinet.

6. In this mode of transacting business, the King met with no restraint in using his Royal authority, and to do every thing he pleased. I was of opinion, and had always heard, that in a sovereign state, the form of government should, as much as possible, be simple, and void of all perplexity. Good principles and the desire of doing justice, are the best means to withhold a Monarch from abusing the power vested in him; other impediments often hinder the execution of great and use-

ful

ful undertakings, without preventing the confequences of a bad application of that fovereign power.

7. All orders from the Cabinet, ever fince I was
Prime Minifter, were directed and fent to the
prefidents and the boards of the different departments; they had the liberty to remon-
ftrate againft them, particularly when they
were found contradictory to the eftablifhed
laws and cuftoms, or in the leaft affecting
previous Royal refolutions.

8. I acquired no perfonal authority by the order
of July 15, but what originated from, and
was limited by the continuance of the confidence his Majefty was pleafed to place in
me.

9. By thefe different regulations, I alfo deprived
myfelf of all means of making the King's
confidence inftrumental to further any private
views of my own, that might in the leaft be
detrimental to his Majefty's intereft and welfare. And if I had had any fuch fecret
fchemes as are laid to my charge (though I
am confcious of my innocence in this refpect)
they might eafily be difcovered from my tranfactions, and from the regifters that remain in
the Cabinet, and I am ready and willing,
when called upon, to give an account of
every thing that even wears the fmalleft appearance thereof.

10. With regard to my fignature to the orders
from the Cabinet, feveral perfons, and particularly the Privy-Counfellor *Schumacher*, were
perfectly acquainted with his Majefty's fentiments upon that fubject; and this was the

only

only reafon, why *not all* orders from the cabinet
were figned by the King himfelf.

Though I have thus declared with the greateft
fincerity, and according to my beft remem-
brance, to what intentions and purpofes I have
made ufe of his Majefty's confidence, yet I will
not take upon me to judge, how far the confequences of my adminiftration, and the different
alterations that were made, have been advantageous or prejudicial to the ftate. Time would
have determined this queftion; but the time it
exifted was too fhort. This, however, I may
venture to affert, that the œconomical regulations at court, and all that is connected therewith, as alfo thofe adopted in regard to his Majefty's privy-purfe, will prove advantageous and
be productive of confiderable favings; that the
regulations of the finances are built upon found
principles, the price of grain throughout the
kingdom, during the laft winter, has fufficiently
proved; that all expences for the fupport of
government of the laft year have been paid,
and the means and ways to raife them have not
been oppreffive to the nation; that the regulations of the different departments, chanceries,
and courts of juftice will be found ufeful; that
thofe perfons, whom I have propofed to different
employments, (two or three excepted, where I
may have been miftaken) were properly qualified for the offices they were appointed to;
and laftly, that no flownefs and negligence has
reigned in the tranfaction of bufinefs. It was
impoffible to avoid, that here and there a fault
might be committed, which though I perceived it, yet it was out of my power to rectify

it

it immediately. If in thefe changes, fome perfons have fuffered, my intention has always been
that they fhould be employed again in offices for
which they were more properly qualified, than
for thofe from which they had been removed,
and that their loffes fhould be made good by
fome means or other. In fhort, if fome of my
undertakings have mifcarried, either by adopting improper meafures, or for want of due fupport, or that, according to the nature and fituation of circumftances, the defeat of them was in-
evitable, I willingly fubmit to all reproaches and
blame that can be thrown out againft me. It is
fufficient, that it has not been executed.

His Majefty alone can decide, what influence
my advices had upon his perfonal happinefs and
wellfare, and a due inveftigation of this point,
will eafily fhew, how far the confequences thereof have been prejudicial to the whole. At firft I
was much encouraged by my friends; but afterwards, when it was too late for me to withdraw,
with any degree of propriety, they left me. If
it were poffible, in a fituation like mine, to act
without any perfonal or private views and par-
tiality, no one can deny that I have endeavoured
to do it; and for fo much the lefs I thought to
deferve a general hatred. For this reafon I was
quite indifferent about all threats and invectives
that were publicly thrown out againft me, and I
never expected that I fhould be accufed of having
employed unlawful means to maintain myfelf in
the fituation I was in, even againft his Majefty's
will and intention; or, what is ftill worfe, of having
had any dangerous views againft his Majefty. I do
not know whether the King ever wifhed, or had
thought of removing me from his perfon, at leaft
I had

I had no reason to believe that he ever did. All that I could do, to maintain myself in the King's favour, was, that I endeavoured, as much as laid in my power, to make myself useful and agreeable to him; and his good opinion, and the influence and interest of the Queen, were the only supports I could depend upon.

Count *Brandt* had lost much of the King's confidence during the last six months, and I had no particular connection with the state counsellor *Reverdil*, who was then in favour, and who certainly would not have suffered himself to be made instrumental in supporting me by any unlawful means. Baron *Schak*, who was then gentleman of the King's bed-chamber, I only knew by sight, before he was placed at court, and professor *Berger* came but seldom before the King; besides these, all the attendants that were about his Majesty before I came to court, were there still, and under no manner of obligation to me. These persons can bear witness, whether I ever desired any advice of what the King had spoken with them, or whether I ever requested any other services to my advantage from them. If I have now and then expressed my wish, that the King might not suffer himself to be led by insinuations, to take a sudden resolution with regard to myself, I thought it very necessary, because there were innumerable opportunities for such insinuations, which I neither could, nor have endeavoured to prevent; and because the resistance I expected they would find in his Majesty's mind, was the only protection I relied upon; as otherwise I should certainly have endeavoured to secure to myself the affection and friendship of those persons, that were constantly about the King. But befides

fides this, his Majesty had found proper means to free himself of several persons that had been about him, so that it would have been an easy matter to do the same with me; and how could I have opposed myself against his resolution?

The other accusation, namely, that I had dangerous views against the person of his Majesty, is likewise ill-grounded and improbable. All and every one prejudiced against me, without any friends or party, and those that were supposed such, equally hated by the public, how could I have thought of any such undertaking? And if this had been my intentions, is it probable that I should have adopted such bad measures? All my security consisted in the King's person and authority; and whose authority could have been substituted in lieu of that of his Majesty's? The regulations that gave rise to this suspicion, were scarcely sufficient, even under the King's immediate authority, to quell an uproar of the people, if any disturbances had happened; how much less would it have been possible to make them active, without such authority, to execute a scheme that must inevitably displease the nation. There is at least no political probability in all this, that such a thought ever existed; and I do not see upon what moral principles the suspicion against those persons, who certainly must have had some knowledge thereof, can be grounded, that they should have been guilty of supporting such a detestable scheme. A close examination of their actions and behaviour, will, I am persuaded, rather prove that they entertained very opposite sentiments towards his Majesty's person. This I cannot deny, that I thought it necessary that preparations should be

made

made, to oppofe the violent undertakings of the rabble, in cafe any fuch fhould have been attempted; and I do not believe, that it is more prudent in any government, to undertake changes in the form of its adminiftration without fuch precautions, than it would be to attempt the execution thereof folely by thefe means.

Thus, I hope, that on a clofe examination of what I have here mentioned, confiftent with the ftricteft truth, of my fentiments, and the motives and principles of my actions, more political miftakes or moral errors, than real punifhable crimes (excepting the only one, of which I have made no mention here, and for which I am full of the fincereft repentance) will be found in my conduct. Thofe who have known me, and clofely obferved my proceedings, may judge whether I have faithfully adhered to the line of ftrict veracity. If riches, diftinctions, or other perfonal advantages had been the chief aim of my purfuits, the fituation I was in offered me much eafier means to obtain them, than the way I chofe. The defire of making my fortune was a far more diftant incitement in my mind; for I would only be indebted for all advantages that might derive for me from my labours, to the fervices I fhould be able to render to the King and the country. My readinefs, implicitly to execute every thing the King wifhed for, and his Majefty's condefcenfion to accept willingly of my advices, cannot entirely juftify me, but they may at leaft ferve to excufe me, in cafe bad confequences for the King's intereft fhould have been the refult of them.

I

I ap-

I appeal to his Majesty's recollection and sensibility, to decide, whether the different changes, which I have either executed, or have been the cause of, have made any disagreeable impressions upon his mind; and I know of no confusion that has resulted, or at least could be derived from them; for the discontent of a few persons can be no decision in this. I was always of opinion, and acted according to that principle, that to the King alone I was beholden to give an account of my actions; and how easy was it for his Majesty to be thoroughly acquainted therewith, and to have the least doubt that might occur properly cleared up, especially as all affairs came so many different times under his immediate inspection. No traces will be found, that I have ever endeavoured to influence the propositions or remonstrances of the different departments, or that I have willingly misrepresented any affairs whatsoever; for every commissioner of the different boards had, in my time, his Majesty's permission to subjoin his own separate remarks to every thing that came from that board into the Cabinet.

The first changes took place among those who chiefly surrounded his Majesty's person, and it would certainly not have been very prudent to begin with the Privy-Council, or the different alterations at court, if his Majesty's own conviction, will and approbation, had not entirely coincided therewith. No one has been forbidden the court, except Count *Laurwig*; nor has any one quitted Copenhagen by order of his Majesty, or been prohibited from coming there; neither has any of the former ministers of state ever been denied an audience

with

with the King. All thofe who had for flight transfgreffions, or through aitful infinuations, incurred his Majefty's difgrace, and had either been arrefted, or forbidden the court and the capital, have, at my interceffion, been releafed and obtained pardon.

Only one particular law-fuit has been protected and decided in the Cabinet; and the caufe between Count *Rantzau* and the Agent *Bodenhoff* can ferve for an example, that no retrofpect upon perfons concerned in an action ever influenced the decifion thereof. Whenever in matters of contract with the King, or relating to impofts, duties, taxes, or other affairs, his Majefty decided upon a caufe, either according to the reprefentation of the department to which the matter related, or to his own conviction, thofe who thought themfelves injured by fuch Royal refolutions, had full liberty to feek redrefs according to the common courfe of the Law. I believe not, that any one can difcover in all this the leaft appearance of a propenfity to defpotifm, no more than in what has happened with regard to fome perfons having been difmiffed from their places. Defpotifm, in my opinion, confifts in a Monarch's knowing no other law than his will, and in arbitraily difpofing of the rights, privileges, lives and properties of his fubjects, without any examination or form of trial whatfoever. Thofe perfons, who loft their places in confequence of the different changes in the departments, received proportionable penfions until they could be employed again on the firft opportunity. The difmiffion of others, at the defire of the different departments to which they belonged,

on

on account of either neglect, infidelity, or any other transgression, rendered, in my opinion, a judicial enquiry totally unnecessary, unless their misdemeanours deserved more rigorous punishment, and yet, in all cases, it was at the option of every one, who thought himself ill treated by the respective departments, to make his complaint in due form.

Concerning the fraud, of which I have been accused, with regard to the instrument to prove the receiving of 60,000 rixdollars of the King, I declare by every thing sacred, that in executing that instrument, I neither intended nor committed any fraud; but that I wrote the very identical sums, which now appear upon that instrument, in the King's presence, before he signed it; and that I expressly requested of his Majesty, for count *Brandt* and myself, the sum of 50,000 rixdollars each, which his Majesty granted, without shewing the least mark of reluctance in giving his consent to these sums, either at the moment of my request, or when he signed the instrument.

In the same solemn manner, I also declare, that whatever I have mentioned with regard to the principles, causes, or views of my actions, and the events in which I have been concerned, have been here represented conformable to the strictest truth, and as far as my memory and knowledge would permit. It does not become me, nor is this a proper place to say any thing in defence of my moral conduct, or of whatever may be foreign to affairs of administration. I have therefore cautiously avoided saying any thing that might be considered as a justification of myself in that light.

I think

, I think it neceffary before I conclude, to mention the following particulars relative to the education of his Royal Highnefs the young Prince of
Denmark. The principles upon which this method of education was regulated, were in every
refpect conformable to the King's ideas, and the
Queen wifhed and defired it, and undertook herfelf the execution thereof. I cannot deny, that I
alfo found them in every refpect proper and advantageous. The Prince, before this mode was
adopted, was of a very delicate conftitution, much
inclined to be ricketty, very capricious, cried often,
would not walk, but always be carried or fitting;
he attached himfelf to particular perfons, would
not play or be diverted, but by noife, finging or
dancing; and he had been infpired with a dread of
her Majefty, by the continual threats of thofe who
attended him, that Mamma was coming, if he
would not behave prettily. To obviate all thefe
abfurdities, as alfo to mend the Prince's health
and manners as much as poffible, the following
means were adopted. His Royal Highnefs was
confined to a fimple diet, fuch as fruit, bread,
water, rice, milk, and in the latter times, potatoes, and every thing cold. In the beginning
he was bathed twice or thrice a week, and at laft
he went every day, on his own accord, to the
cold bath. During the two laft winters he was
kept in a cold room, unlefs when he was with his
Royal Mother. He was but lightly clothed, and,
during the laft winter, moftly without fhoes or
ftockings. He had permiffion to do what he pleafed,
and to have all what he could obtain by his own
abilities; but when he cried, or obftinately demanded
any thing, which was not thought proper or neceffary
for him to have, it was refufed him, but he re-

ceived

ceived no punishment, reproach or threats, nor
any promises to quiet him. When he fell down,
he was left to get up by himself, and the servants had
orders neither to assist or reprimand him, or suffer
him to discover in them the least marks of affright.
A playfellow, much of the same age and disposition was given him, who in every respect was
treated like himself I hey were generally left to
play by themselves, and at their meals, their dress-
ing and undressing, they assisted each other. They
clambered, broke, and did what they pleased; but
particular care was taken that nothing should remain within their reach, wherewith they might do
themselves an injury. When the one either hurted
or afronted the other, they were left to make it up
between themselves, and the servants had strict
charge not to interfere, nor to speak or play with
them. His Royal Highness's learning was to begin in his sixth or seventh year; and till then it
was thought adviseable to leave his ideas and con-
ceptions in some measure uncontrouled. The result of all this has been, that the constitution of
the Prince is now as robust and confirmed, as can
be expected in an infant of his age. His Royal
Highness has been, since that time, a few instances
excepted, as healthy as could be wished. He has
undergone the operation of inoculation with the
greatest ease and success; he perfectly knows the
use of his limbs, as far as is consistent with his
age; he dresses and undresses himself, goes up and
down stairs without assistance, and knows how
cautiously to avoid accidents. He is no longer
alarmed by those fears, which often arise from ab-
surd threats and warnings. He is not bashful, capricious, nor has the least remains of his former
humours. Whoever requires no uncommon capacity

pacity, or confummate politenefs, will find the
Prince no ways deficient in what can be expected
from a child of five years of age. If it be advantageous that a Prince fhould have the firft education
common with other men, that he fhould receive
that ftrength of body which is never derived from a
delicate education; that he fhould know how to affift
himfelf in his little perfonal neceffities, without entirely depending on the help of others; that he
fhould not too foon be apprifed of the dignity
he was born to, in order that it might not become
a burthen, or infpire him with pride, which muft
afterwards be checked by moral principles; if,
finally, that early education is deemed the beft,
which is the moft natural, I believe that no one
will find that adopted with the Prince in any degree to be cenfured. The only punifhments made
ufe of were, that he either was deprived of his
breakfaft, or left in a room by himfelf, when he
committed any material fault.

Perhaps it may not be fuperfluous here to fub-
join a more pofitive declaration of my fentiments
with regard to the treaty of alliance with Ruffia I
have always been of opinion, that the King might
adhere to it; and though I was not at firft fully
convinced of the advantages of the Holftein negociation, I have notwithftanding advifed, not to
liften to any other propofitions, in order cautioufly
to avoid all fufpicion at the court of Peterfburgh.
The infinuations and opinions of others, and particularly of Count *Rantzau*, have made but little
impreffion on me, nor have I paid any attention
thereto. Thefe aimed chiefly at not folely to depend on the court of Peterfburgh, but to form connections with other ftates, and particularly with

I 4   the

the court of Sweden. I have never obferved an inclination thereto in General *Gahler*, and ever fince
laft Eafter I have fpoken with no one concerning
this matter, except with the minifter of the foreign department. With regard to the affair with
Sweden, I thought it advantageous that the King
fhould take no other part in it, than was confiftent
with the Ruffian treaty; but feek no other influence by any means, and particularly by money.

These are the principles according to which I
have acted in this affair, though I have fometimes
faid, that the alliance with Ruffia was not
the only refource for Denmark, and that it was
not proper to facrifice every other confideration to
that alone.

12 JY 62

Struenfee.

THE
JUDGMENT

OF THE

ROYAL COMMISSION

OF

INQUISITION,

UPON THE

PLEA OF THE ATTORNEY-GENERAL,

As PLAINTIFF for the CROWN,

AGAINST

COUNT JOHN FRED. STRUENSEE,

D E F E N D A N T.

Given at the CASTLE of CHRISTIANSBURGH,

A P R I L 25, 1772.

TOGETHER WITH

THE ROYAL APPROBATION.

THE

JUDGMENT, &c.

THOUGH Count *John Frederick Stru-enfee,* now ſtands lawfully and indubitably convicted, and has himſelf confeſſed, of having been guilty of a *certain atrocious crime,* (*) at the bare recital of which human nature ſhudders, and which the faultering tongue ſeems unwilling to repeat;—a *crime,* which has ſullied the unblemiſhed honour, glory, and dignity of the Royal Houſe, and which, according to the eſtabliſhed Law, (Book VI. Chap. iv. Art. 1.) ought to be puniſhed with all the aggravated horrors of death;—though this crime alone is in every reſpect ſufficient to juſtify the ſentence he will ſpeedily receive, yet we think it our duty, cautiouſly to examine the validity of the other crimes laid to his charge by the Attorney-General, and to enumerate them here, according as we find them proved and authenticated, either by his own confeſſion, by the declaration of ſeveral witneſſes examined upon oath, or by original inſtruments now upon the Records before us.

From

(*) See the Attorney-General's Accuſation, Sect. I. p, 26.

From thefe we find it clearly proved, that Count *Struenfee*'s conduct, during the time he had any fhare in the management of public affairs, was impetuous, wanton, and prefump-tuous. Every fpecies of hypocritical cunning and deceit were by him put in practice, in order to procure to himfelt an unlimitted power and authority, in preference to, and exclufive of all others. To attain this end, nothing feemed too facred to ftop his career, fince he fported with the Conftitution, and trampled on the ancient form of Government, and the fundamental laws of the Empire.

The principal points he aimed at, were the place of Prime Minifter, with the extraordinary and unheard of authority, which he afterwards furreptitioufly obtained in the month of July, 1771; to keep the King from his fubjects, and the fubjects from their Sovereign; and to rule with unlimitted fway and fuch arbitrary power over the empire, the court, and even the Mo-narch himfelf, as filled the mind of every fub-ject with horror, aftonifhment and furprife.

In order to fucceed in this inglorious attempt, he eagerly grafped every favourable opportunity that offered, during the King's journey abroad, to infinuate himfelf into his favour, by affiduity in his attendance, and the diligent care he took in all that concerned his Majefty's health and pleafure. On the King's return, *Struenfee*, lived quietly and contentedly at court, defired no aug-mentation to his falary, and feemed not to har-bour in his bofom the leaft anxiety for riches and honours.—But, at the fame time, he was fecretly laying the foundation, upon which he meant to erect the edifice of his future grandeur. The

language

language, conftitution, and fundamental Laws of
the country; the cuftoms, and the natural and
commercial interefts of the nation, of which he
fhould have endeavoured to acquire a thorough
knowledge, in cafe he meant to fucceed in his
ambitious attempt,—thefe he looked upon as
trifles unworthy of his attention. His conftant
ftudy was to find out the ruling paffions of the
King, and to what form of government he was at
heart inclined. From this difcovery he fuppofed
he fhould be the better enabled to forward his
diabolical fchemes, which as yet were only in
embrio. But, as fear and jealoufy perpetually
haunt the guilty foul, fo *Struenfee* plainly perceived, that he could not proceed with fecurity,
unlefs he could remove from his Majefty all his
old and faithful fervants, and place the tools of
his choice in their room. To hinder, therefore,
that either fome true friends to their country
might difcover his views, or that the King himfelf might perceive them, he, to prevent the firft,
endeavoured to prejudice his Majefty againft all
thofe who had the honour of approaching his
royal perfon; and to fecure himfelf againft the
latter, he procured, by the moft *illicit* and *deteftable* means, a powerful protection in the
Queen, and placed a trufty friend by the King,
whofe bufinefs it was, to praife and to reprefent
all *Struenfee's* actions in the moft advantageous
light, and to hinder all others from approaching
his Majefty, fo that it was impoffible for the King
to fee through his wicked fchemes.

Thus he imitated, in every refpect, the firft
ftep of evil and corrupt minifters. they carefully
block up every avenue to the Throne, poifon the
mind of their Sovereign, and bring him to treat

with

with indifference and contempt, the remonstrances of an oppressed people, even should their complaints by chance reach his royal ear. This point *Struensee* most effectually and unhappily obtained; and having compleatly formed his destructive machine, in the year 1770, he immediately gave to it motion.

Our Kings, ever since they were entrusted with Sovereignty, have kept a Privy-Council, which confisted of men of extensive knowledge and experience, who were thoroughly acquainted with the laws, constitution, and the true interest of both kingdoms; who were trained up in the study and practice of politics and state business; who knew the system of government, and the maxims to be adopted on different occasions. It was their peculiar province to assist his Majesty with their advice, whenever matters of importance were laid before him for his decision, and whenever the King should require their opinion. They had otherwise, as members of the Privy-Council, no vote, no power, nor secretary; for every thing depended upon the will of the Sovereign, and all business was transacted in the offices of the different departments.

This Council, whose institution was ancient and confonant with the nature of the government, was an obstacle to the views of *Struensee*, who therefore determined to have it dissolved. For he feared, that should it exist, even if composed of his own creatures; yet the time might come, when, having established themselves in the confidence of their Sovereign, and grown weary of supporting his tyrannical and iniquitous schemes, they might perhaps throw off the mask, and expose them to the eyes of the King. *Struensee* well knew,

knew, that no confidence is to be placed in traitors.

To this end, he made ufe of the implicit confidence he had gained over his Sovereign, to the bafeft purpofes. every trifling miftake of the miniftry was magnified to the higheft degree, while every meritorious proceeding, though it undeniably tended to the advantage of the King and the ftate, was either buried in oblivion, or falfely reprefented, as being detrimental to his Majefty's intereft.

The King, who fincerely loves his people, and therefore expects reciprocal attachment and fidelity in his fervants, and who cannot bear incroachments on his prerogative, infenfibly loft all confidence to his Privy-Council, and refolved to give it a new form, and to name other members thereto. But we find that *Struenfee*, by his artful machinations, oppofed fo many obftacles to his Majefty's views, that the Privy-Council was at laft formally diffolved by an edict of December 27, 1770.

At the fame time he was appointed chief private fecretary to his Majefty; and, as his plan was to arrogate all power to himfelf, and to be the King's fole counfellor in all affairs of ftate, he foon perceived that the chief officers of the different departments formed another obftacle to his views. To remove this alfo, he propofed to his Majefty, who always wifhed to be thoroughly informed of all matters laid before him by the different departments for his decifion, and which had always been done in an audience with the prefident of that board to which the affair related, that nothing would anfwer the purpofe better, than his Majefty giving orders, that, for the future, the

the different departments fhould make their reports, and give their opinion in writing, that his
Majefty might have time to read and examine
them more maturely, and give his decifion accordingly. By this plaufible, and in appearance
fo ufeful advice, this iniquitous man fucceeded in
his undertaking, to feparate the King from his
fervants and fubjects, and the different departments from the ear of the Sovereign. He foon
made himfelf mafter of all reports, papers, &c.
which, according to this order were fent to the
Cabinet, and reprefented matters to the King as
he thought moft conducive to his private views.
Thus he became equal at leaft, if not fuperior,
to what the whole body of the Privy-Council,
and all the officers of the different departments
of ftate had been before.

Under the fpecious pretext of haftening the
difpatch of fome particular bufinefs, and to fhew
the King's authority, he often iffued orders from
the Cabinet, and caufed them to be executed,
even before the department, under whofe cognizance the affair fhould have fallen, had any notice thereof. This occafioned immenfe trouble
and confufion; and inftead of difpatching, hindered the regular courfe of bufinefs.

The different departments, which before had
tranfacted all bufinefs in the Danifh language,
were now under the neceffity of appointing inter-
preters, to tranflate every thing into the German
language, that Count *Struenfee* might be enabled to read it (*). The Danifh chancery, which

was

(*) That Count *Struenfee* was not well aequainted with
the Danifh language, fufficiently appears in his having made
his defence in German. from which language, as we before
obferved, we have tranflated it.

was the only department that continued to tranfact bufinefs in the Danifh language, had often occafion to obferve, that their reprefentations, re-
quefts, &c. were either totally difregarded or
mifunderftood, becaufe Count *Struenfee* read nothing but the extract, which, according to order,
was with all poffible brevity, to be fubjoined to
every paper, and which was tranflated into the
German language, whereupon the refolution from
the Cabinet was likewife given in the German,
and in the Chancery was again tranflated into
Danifh. Under thefe circumftances, it is natural
to fuppofe, that many blunders muft unavoidably have happened. Affairs, which required
the greateft nicety and punctuality, were often
rendered doubtful and obfcure, and frequently
totally perverted. Every difcerning mind muft
feel for the wretched adminiftration of that
period. The King judged of every thing from
the reprefentations of *Struenfee*, who feldom underftood the nature of the bufinefs itfelf; and
therefore it often happened, that the very reverfe
of the King's will and pleafure was executed,
owing to improper expreffions, or errors in the
tranflation of the Royal refolutions.

Private perfons, who had any petitions, or
other bufinefs to prefent to the Cabinet, were
likewife under the neceffity of having every thing
tranflated into German, the confequence of which
frequently was, that thefe tranflations, being obtained at a low price, were executed in fo mife-
rable a manner, that the utmoft limits of human
knowledge could not reach at their meaning.
Hence the bufinefs was either retarded, or entirely difmiffed, to the great detriment of the
individuals concerned therein.

K   The

The ignorance of Count *Struensee*, with regard to the interior regulations of the different departments of state; his indolence in not acquiring any knowledge thereof, and his desire to abolish the ancient form of government, and to augment the number of his adherents, whom he placed every where in the highest and most lucrative posts without regarding their want of abilities for those important offices,—these induced him to new model one department after another. And as he himself had neither the abilities nor inclination to do much business, he always employed other persons in these important charges, who were as ignorant as himself, and many of whom have themselves confessed, that they had not, nor endeavoured to acquire, the least knowledge of the established form of government, and the nature, merits, or defects of the interior regulations of its departments; but that they have acted in conformity to the general order they received, namely, to draw up a plan for new regulations, according to certain fixed principles.

After Count *Struensee* had thus arrogated to himself all power and authority, by dissolving the Privy-Council, enervating and new modelling the different departments of state, and excluding them from the conferences with their Sovereign, the nation soon felt the consequences, and groaned under the weight of his arbitrary and despotic principles.

The tender hand, with which Denmark has ever held the reins of government, has inspired every subject with such a sense of that blessing, that, through length of time, it is become so natural to them, that they now seem to claim it as a right. Hence those who held any employment

under

under his Majefty had drawn this certain conclufion, that while induftry, care and integrity,
guided their fteps, they fhould never feel the
weight of his Majefty's difpleafure, or be deprived of thofe pofts they poffeffed, unlefs legally
convicted of fome mifdemeanour, neglect, or
incapacity.

Thefe maxims, which were the refult of the
mild difpofition of our Sovereigns, and which
have, in many inftances, had the moft falutary
effects, were not at all confonant with the
principles of *Struenfee*, who never put himfelf
under any conftraint whenever he had one of his
creatures to provide for. Examples of this nature have been daily given, and with the utmoft
regret we have feen old and faithful fervants
turned out, and others put in their places, without
the former ever knowing the caufe of their difgrace. Thefe cruelties were not only exercifed on
individuals of different rank and ftation, but even
againft whole affemblies.

The whole body of Magiftrates of Copenhagen, which confifted of upwards of 20 members, was difmiffed, and another appointed,
without alledging any reafon for fuch proceeding,
or ufing any other formality, than an order from
the Cabinet, dated April 3, 1771, and addreffed
to the new prefident, who likewife, a few days
before, had been named to that office, in the
room of another, and who acquainted the former
members, in a letter, that they were difmiffed,
and the new ones, that they were to appear at the
town-houfe. -

Befides thefe Magiftrates, there was another affembly, which confifted of thirty-two of the principal citizens, chofen by, and from the whole body of

the

the freemen of Copenhagen, called the *Common-Council of the thirty-two citizens*. The institution of this assembly (on June 24, 1664) was considered as a valuable privilege granted to the city of Copenhagen, as a reward for the loyalty and affection of the citizens towards their Sovereign, and for their integrity, courage, and bravery, during the siege of Copenhagen, and on the establishment of the Sovereignty in Denmark. This Common-Council, in conjunction with the Magistrates, had the management of all civil affairs in the city, and the advantages arising from this body of men, who, while they promoted the prosperity of the corporation, were no burthen to either the revenue or the city, justly entitled them to the thanks and veneration of their fellow citizens, and the prerogative they enjoyed with the other Magistrates, of being occasionally admitted into the presence of the Sovereign. This assembly also became obnoxious to the views of Count *Struensee*, and was therefore likewise dissolved by the said order from the Cabinet, without any other formality, than that the president acquainted the members they should assemble no more, and ordered their council-chamber to be locked up.

These, and other such like proceedings, sufficiently shewed, that nothing was capable of stopping the arbitrary career of this hateful man, who seemed to hold justice, lenity, prudence and good order, in contempt, and who aimed at the unlimitted power of an Eastern tyrant.

It is easily imagined what effects this produced in the minds of the subjects. Some sighed at, and lamented the oppression of their country; others expressed their astonishment and anger in

different

diffeient ways; but all agreed in this one point, that his Majesty had still the same kind and paternal affection for his people, and would certainly redress their grievances, could but the voice of oppieffion reach the throne, and the King be made acquainted with the true situation of the empire. But this seemed abiolutely impracticable; for *Struerfe* had so posted the iniquituous tools of his gloomy designs, that no passage to the throne was left open.

He had placed, as a guard over the King, his trusty friend *Brandt*, whose business it was, to praise and approve whatever *Struenfee* propofed, to take care that none approached his Majesty, but those in whom *Struenfee* thought he could confide; and, when at any time the contrary happened, it was only for a moment; so that his Majesty was constantly kept a stranger to the true state of affairs, and the oppreffions his fubjects laboured under. This exclufion fiom the King's presence was even extended to perfons of the Royal Family, for whom the King had al. ays before manifested the greatest love and affection. But fince Count *Struenfee* had arrogated to himfelf the government of the court and the state, they came but feldom to the King, and care was then taken, that they should find no opportunity to converfe with him in private, as otherwife they certainly would not have neglected to reprefent to his Majesty the lamentable state of the empire, and to ufe their endeavous to redref the grievances of the nation; of which zeal for the welfare of the fubjects, thefe high perfons gave afterwaids, when they found a proper opportu nity, fuch convincing proofs, as can never be fufficiently praifed and admired.

K 3

Such

Such arbitrary, defpotic, and tyrannical principles, as were evident in every meafure adopted
by Count *Struenfee*, could not fail to draw on him
the moft fincere and heart-felt imprecations of the
whole nation. His tools and adherents, though
they dared not to juftify, nor could with any
degree of juftice, applaud or palliate his meafures,
yet they at leaft endeavoured to extol his affected
moderation, and reprefented him as a man, who
lived contentedly on his falary, without feeking
riches or honours, either for himfelf or his friends.

What degree of credit was given to thefe reports is needlefs to examine. Certain however
it is, that Count *Struenfee*, though he at firft cau-
t oufly concealed from the world the avaricious
principles implanted in his foul; yet no fooner
d d he think himfelf fecure in his ufurped ftation,
then it was plainly feen, that the love of plunder
and rapine was likewife one of his ruling paffions,
and to glut this he even fhunned not to rob his
Majefty's coffers

His falary was very confiderable, and the more
fufficient, as he lived at court, free of all expences,
even in the fumptuous feafts and banquets he
often gave to his friends. And notwithftanding
he was well acquainted with the bad ftate of the
finances, which he even reported abroad to be
worfe than they really were; yet fcarce had he
been three months in office, after the privy-
council was diffolved, when he feized the favourable opportunity of the King's good humour,
to requeft and accept a prefent of 10000 rixdollars for himfelf, and the like fum for his
friend *Brandt*.

Every reafonable perfon will fuppofe, that fo
confiderable a prefent fhould have fatisfied the ex-
pectations

pectations of thefe men for fome time at leaft; but their avarice proved infatiable, and the encreafe of riches only promoted their more fanguine purfuit of them. Hence, having received thefe prefents in February or March, Count *Struenfee* found means, in the month of May following, to procure for himfelf and Count *Brardt* another fum of 50, or 60,000 rixdollars each, and thus thefe avaricious men, who both had been but a fhort time in office, coft his Majefty in the courfe of only three or four months, above 140,000 rixdollars, befides their fettled falary, and without mentioning the feveral prefents they procured for their adherents, as for inftance, to Count *Struenfee*'s brother 4000 rixdollars; to the Countefs of *Helftein* 3000; to Col. *Falkenfchiold* 3500, (*) and many others.

That Count *Struenfee* was abfolutely determined to make his fortune at the expence of the *Danifh* nation, appears alfo plainly from his artful contrivances to get at leaft fome of the King's money under his immediate direction, by which means he was enabled to appropriate to his own ufe what fums he pleafed, without the knowledge of any one.

With this view he propofed to his Majefty, to take up the private treafure (which confifted in a fum of money that had been long laid afide to fupply the wants of fudden and unexpected exigencies) and to deliver it into the general treafury. But when the neceffary orders for this were preparing in the Cabinet, he again propofed to the King, to take 250,000 rixdollars from that private

K 4　　　　trea-

(*) A *Danifh* rixdollar is equivalent to about four fhillings *Englifh* money; fo that the whole of thefe fums amounted nearly to 30,100l. fterling.

reafure, and to eftablifh a Special Cabinet Treafury, for private fervices, which was to be entirely
under his direction

From hence Count *Struenfee* obtained the accom-
plifhment of his wifhes, to appropriate to himfelf
any fums he thought proper; and, indeed, he failed not to take every advantage of this favourable
opportunity: for this Special Cabinet Treafury being eftablifhed in the month of April, 1771, and
confifting then of 250,000 rixdollars, there remained no more, at the end of May following,
than 118,000 rixdollars, though not a fingle fhil-
ling had been applied towards the exigencies of
the ftate.

Count *Strueufee*'s felfifhnefs and avarice are ftill
more confpicuous in this and the following proceedings, and fhew that his thirft after riches has
been fo great, that he fhunned not to commit the
moft deteftable crimes, fuch as fraud and robbery,
to fatisfy his paffion.

When the accounts he kept of this Special Cabinet Treafury, which were found amongft his
papers, and which appearing fufpicious, were laid
before his Majefty, the King immediately declared,
that he well remembered his having given at that
time 10,000 rixdollars to his royal confort, and to
both Counts *Struenfee* and *Brandt* 6000 rixdollars
each, but nothing more. Thefe fums taken together, produce 22,000 rixdollars, which is the
very original fum that feems to have appeared upon the inftrument when the King approved thereof by his own fignature, and which was afterwards altered into 132,000, by changing the firft
figure of 2, into a 3, (which is fo apparent and
clear, that no one, who fees the original inftru-
ment, can in the leaft doubt of it) and by prefix-

in

ing the figure of 1, for which there was no other room than before the line drawn downwards on the paper, to separate the context from the sums, which is not only unusual, but also contrary to what has been observed in the preceding accounts, and particularly in the page just before, where the receipt of the sum of 250,000 rixdollars is entered, and all the figures regularly placed between their proper lines. To make the produce of this total sum, the two preceding sums of 6000, were, by adding a nullo, changed into 60,000; and to hinder the alteration of the second figure of 2, in the total sum, another sum of 2000 rixdollars was added for Colonel *Falkenschiold*, which with the 10,000 for the Queen, make just the sum of 132,000 rixdollars.

The certainty of this fraud, which will clearly appear to every one who sees the original instrument, by the difference in the writing and ink, by the irregularity in which the figures are placed, &c. is farther confirmed by the following circumstances: *First*, the accounts for the two months of April and May are written by Count *Struensee* himself, whereas all the preceding accounts, extracts, &c. are written by the secretary in the Cabinet; which seems to have been done with a view to conceal this fraud from the knowledge of every one. *Secondly*, no state of accounts was laid before his Majesty, till the end of October following, in hopes, that after such a distance of time, the King would neither remember, nor closely examine the true state of the Special Cabinet Treasury: And *Thirdly*, it is not probable, (as the King has himself observed) that his Majesty should have given to *Struensee* and *Brandt* 50, or 60,000 rixdollars each, when he gave only 10,000 to the Queen.

Count

Count *Struenfee*, who indeed could not deny his avarice in demanding fuch prefents, has however endeavoured to evade the fraud by faying, that he actually did follicit 50,000 rixdollars for himfelf, and the like fum for Count *Brandt*, which his Majefty had granted; and as the 10,000 rixdollars they had before received, had no where been brought to account, he had here mentioned the whole under one head. But notwithftanding all thefe allegations, when the original inftrument was laid before him in court, he could not help confeffing himfelf, that all circumftances concurred to give it the appearance of a wilful and premeditated fraud, from which he could by no means clear himfelf; and that he had reafon to repent his irregularity and negligence.

His ambition for places of honour, feems to have been full as great and predominant in his bofom, as his paffion and defire for riches; he had in two years advanced farther in the road of fortune, than men of greater merit and abilities can reafonably expect to accomplifh in twenty; and the fituation he was in, could not fail to command refpect both from the court and the public: yet all this was not fufficient. He aimed at rank and titles, and by means of his artful infinuations, foon obtained his wifhes. On July 15, 1771, he was declared Prime Minifter of the Cabinet, and foon after he was with his trufty friend *Brandt*, raifed to the dignity of a Danifh Count.

He had already, before his appointment to that important poft, affumed more power and authority, than what was becoming a man in his fituation; and as all thofe who were continually about his Majefty moftly depended on *Struenfee*, the King heard nothing but the continual praife of *Struenfee*'s

merits

merits and fagacity. He himfelf had the good-will and confidence of his royal Mafter; and, as he was the only man who converfed with the King upon ftate bufinefs, and reprefented every thing as he pleafed, it could not fail that his Majefty generally approved of his propofitions. In fhort, he had every thing he could reafonably wifh for, rank, title, riches, and reputation; and yet his troubled foul was not to be hufhed by the calm and ftill voice of contentment. Ambition had raifed fuch a ftorm in his bofom, that nothing could appeafe it but that violent fate which is generally the refult of unbounded pride.

Notwithftanding the Count's being raifed to fuch an exalted ftation and dignity, and looking upon himfelf as the fiift man in the kingdom; yet he was not fatisfied with the bare title and the ufual prerogatives of a Prime Minifter, but would have fuch power and authority connected therewith, as are wholly unbecoming a fubject, and wherewith the Sovereigns of thefe realms only are intrufted.

Some of the departments and great officers of ftate had refufed to execute his commands in affairs of importance, without feeing the King's fignature, as had always been cuftomary. This was fufficient to affront the pride of *Struenfee*, who could not brook the thought of a fuperior, and there were reafons to fuppofe, that he looked upon this as a hinderance to the execution of his fecret fchemes. He therefore defired that his fignature fhould have the fame authority as that of his Majefty, and that all thofe whom it concerned, fhould yield the fame obedience to the one as to the other.

This end he alfo obtained by the fame royal order of July 15, 1771, drawn up by himfelf, whereby he was named Prime Minifter. The firft article

ticle of this order, declares and ordains, " That
" all future orders from the Cabinet, figned by
" Count *Struenfee*, and fealed with the King's
" Cabinet feal, fhall be of the fame force and va-
" lidity, as thofe figned by the King himfelf ;"
and the fourth article exprefsly enjoins, " that all
" and every one fhall yield due obedience to all
" fuch orders figned and iffued by Count *Struen-*
" *fee*." Thus he arrogated to himfelf the fole
fovereign power vefted in the King only ; and by
what had paffed before, every one could judge,
that he intended to execute it alone.

As Count *Struenfee* has confeffed, that he hath
read the laws of this country, and as he, as Prime
Minifter, ought to have been particularly acquainted with them, he therefore could not be ignorant,
that, according to the 7th article, all orders, letters, and other ftate papers, fhall be figned by the
King himfelf ; and that the 26th article pofitively
expreffes and ordains : " That in cafe any one,
" whofoever he may be, fhall, in any manner,
" attempt, obtain, or execute any thing, that
" might in the leaft equal, diminifh, or annoy the
" King's prerogative, fhall, notwithftanding 'all
" and every thing, that might have been faid,
" promifed, or obtained, be confidered as of no
" effect, in any manner whatever, and that he,
" who has attempted, obtained, or executed fuch
" things, fhall be confidered as a traitor to his
" King, and his crime be deemed high treafon
" againft the fole fovereign power of the Monarch,
" and he be punifhed accordingly."

Count *Struenfee* might here, without our proceeding any further, have read his fentence and well-
merited punifhment, though there were no other
equally enormous and atrocious crimes, of which
we

' we find he has been guilty: namely, that he not only knew before, but even advised and planned a moſt horrid attack upon the ſacred perſon of his Majeſty, which was committed by his truſty friend Count *Brandt*, in ſo ſhocking and barbarous a manner, as put the King in corporeal fear, and his life in danger.

The manner in which Count *Struenſee* has executed the power he had arrogated to himſelf, can no ways ſerve to excuſe him, but falls heavy to his charge, becauſe he has in many inſtances acted contrary to his Majeſty's abſolute commands, expreſſed in the *third* article of the ſame order, whereby he received that power.

He has iſſued orders from the Cabinet, under his own hand only, to repeal ancient laws, and former Royal ordonnances.

He has, in the moſt important affairs, iſſued ſuch orders from the Cabinet, without the King's knowledge, and has either not entered them at all in the extracts, which according to the King's abſolute commands of July 15, he was to lay before his Majeſty every week; or when entered, he neglected to lay the extracts before the King in proper time, or elſe has made ſuch extracts, from which it was impoſſible for his Majeſty to gueſs what it properly concerned.

In the ſpring, 1771, he had by his artful inſinuations brought it ſo far, that his Majeſty's horſe-guard (which conſiſted only of two ſquadrons, and therefore could not coſt large ſums) was diſmiſſed, under pretence of ſaving money; notwithſtanding the military department had ſerally remonſtrated againſt theſe proceedings.

The diſbanding of his Majeſty's foot-guard was the next object he aimed at. It conſiſted of five companies, all well-bred and faithful people, who, on account of their experienced attachment to the King and Royal Family, could safely be entrusted with the guard of the Royal palace and apartments. But they had one quality which displeased Count *Struensee*, namely, they were all natives of *Denmark* and *Norway*

He had long resolved within himself to disband this corps, and had mentioned his intention to several of his friends, who mostly endeavoured to dissuade him from from it. At last he threw aside all constraint, and on December 21, 1771, issued, without the King's knowledge (which his Majesty has himself declared) an order from the Cabinet to the military department, according to which, the five companies of foot-guard were to be changed into so many companies of grenadiers, and one company of which was to be subjoined to each of the five regiments then at garrison in Copenhagen.

He also let pass the 21st, 22d, and 23d of December, without mentioning any thing to the King (which his Majesty has also declared to remember perfectly well) till the military department remonstrated against this order, and refused to execute it, unless his Majesty would himself approve of it by his own signature, because they considered it as an affair of importance, and foresaw the consequences that would happen; whereupon *Struensee* accordingly procured the Royal approbation.

But when the guard, on December 24, insisted upon their capitulation being fulfilled, and refused to be incorporated into other regiments, Count *Struensee*, by his artful contrivances, and false representation of the true motive of their disobedience,

dience, procured another Royal order, according to which all thofe, who would not ferve as grenadiers in other regiments, received their difmiffion. The confequences of this operation were, that the King loft feveral hundred well-difciplined and valiant foldiers; and thus many of his Majefty's fubjects, who had long ferved their King and country faithfully, were turned out of their bread.

Count *Struenfee*'s deceitful and hypocritical conduct in this affair is ftill more apparent, on examining the regifters of the Cabinet, where the different orders are entered, and on comparing the fame with the book of extracts. In the regifter, the order of December 21, is entered under the right date, and in its proper place, No. 709. After this follow feveral others of December 22, 23, and 24, until No. 733. But the laft mentioned order of December 24, concerning the difmiffion of the life-guard, is not entered at all, but there is a blank left for it. On the contrary, in the extracts from December 18 till 25, the two orders of December 21 and 24, concerning the life-guard, follow immediately one after the other, under No. 22 and 23, juft as if they had been iffued at the fame time, and under the fame date; but all the other orders, iffued the 22d and 23d, are there left out entirely. From this it is eafy to judge how far his Majefty could be informed of his actions by thefe extracts, and what regularity and order have reigned in all his proceedings.

The fame regifter alfo fhews, that notwithftanding Count *Struenfee* had taken every poffible precaution to prevent his Majefty from receiving any verbal information to his difadvantage, yet,

on

on the difmiffion of the life-guard, he thought it
neceffary to adopt new meafures, to prevent the
fame being done in writing. To this end he iffued two orders from the Cabinet, on December
23 (which are entered in the regifter in their proper places) the one to the ftate counfellor *Waitz*,
at Hamburgh, purporting, that all letters and
packets that came by the poft from foreign countries, fhould be directed to the Cabinet, and the
other to the fteward of his Majefty's houfhold,
commanding that all letters, packets, &c. which
had before been delivered into the King's anti-
chamber, fhould for the future be delivered into
the Cabinet. The one of thefe orders, though
they both materially concerned his Majefty, is
entirely left out in the extracts, and the other is
entered long afterwards, in fo confufed and im-
perfect a manner, that it is impoffible to guefs
the true meaning thereof.

Thefe proceedings fufficiently fhewed, that
Count *Struenfee* was confcious of his ill conduct,
and that he wifhed to conceal it from his Royal
mafter. In this fituation he miftrufted all around
him; and as the hatred of the nations, and the
general difapprobation to all his regulations was
alfo univerfally expreffed in many different ways,
by all ranks of people, he feared that nothing
good awaited him. A difturbance that happened laft fummer among the marines and failors
of his Majefty's navy, who, finding themfelves injured by fome of his new regulations, went in a
body to Hirfhholm, to prefent a petition to the
King, terrified *Struenfee* to fuch a degree, that he
immediately refolved to betake himfelf to flight.
But as fome of his adherents diffuaded him from
that refolution, and this affair taking no ferious

turn,

turn, he determined to maintain himfelf, at all events, in the fituation he had ufurped, and to prevent all fuch further attempts and fears, he adopted fuch meafures as he thought moft proper for his fecurity.

Knowing the general diffatisfaction the citizens of Copenhagen expreffed to all his proceedings, he thought to fecure himfelf, and to keep them in awe, by appointing one of his friends and adherents to the important place of Commander in chief of that city.

He alfo thought the garrifon of Copenhagen too numerous, and therefore ordered, that two regiments fhould be quartered in other cities. Inftead of that lot falling on the two youngeft regiments, according to the opinion and remonftrance of the board of ordonnance, Count *Struenfee* (from motives beft known to himfelf) would have it, that it fhould be the King's own regiment and that of Prince *Frederick*, without ever mentioning a word, or requefting the confent of his Royal Highnefs, as chief of the faid regiment.

Whenever his Majefty came to town, where *Struenfee* generally accompanied him, an uncommon numerous efcort followed them; and whereever his Majefty went, either to the Palace or the Theatre, the guards were always doubled. This exafperated the inhabitants of Copenhagen, who could think no otherwife, but that *Struenfee* either perfuaded his Majefty of fome dangerous defigns amongft them, againft the King and Royal Family, or that he was at the eve of executing fome fecret and pernicious fcheme of his own planning.

But their rage and indignation were at laft roufed to the higheft pitch, on hearing of the new

L   regula-

regulation made by *Struenfee*, and the Commander
in chief of the city, namely, that several loaded
canons, with a sufficient number of hands and
proper ammunition, were kept in constant readinefs for ufe, at a moment's notice; which regulation has always been kept a fecret from his
Majefty.

In fhort, the King and the Royal Family, as
well as the whole nation, at laft loft all patience,
when they faw his cruelty, and daring arrogance,
in the education of his Royal Highnefs the
young Prince of Denmark. The method he
prefcribed for bringing up this Royal infant,
was fo uncommon and inhuman, that his Royal
Highnefs's health and conftitution, nay even his
life, were in many inftances expofed to the moft
imminent danger.

Such were the adminiftration and conduct of a
man, who had not the leaft idea of the art of
government; who was unacquainted with the
language, genius, and manners of a nation,
and totally ignorant of the fundamental laws,
and the natural and commercial intereft of an
empire, over which he undertook to reign as
fole arbiter. This ignorance of Count *Struenfee* in thofe effential points, which it materially
behoves a Minifter of ftate to know, and his
unwillingnefs and neglect to acquire any know-
lege thereof, has been proved, in many inftances,
to have been highly detrimental to the nation
in general, and to individuals in particular.

It therefore could not fail, that difcontent
reigned throughout every part of the nation,
and every mind feemed ripe for open rebellion.
The people were weary of fighing under the
yoke of the arbitrary government of this dar-

ing

ing and ambitious Count, who had shut up all avenues to the throne, to hinder them from laying their grievances before their beloved Sovereign, from whose humanity, benevolence, and tender affection for his people, they might have truly expected immediate redress. All their attempts in this proved however unsuccesful, and, their patience being exhausted, made room for desperation, which would have certainly been followed by the most dreadful consequences, had not the Almighty Disposer of all things hastened the wished-for period that fixed the end of the unnatural proceedings of this vain, imprudent, arbitrary and ambitious minister.

Whereas, therefore, on a strict investigation of the several crimes laid to his charge, a due consideration of what has been said in his defence, and an impartial examination of the evidences, it is clearly, sufficiently, and lawfully proved, that Count *Struensee* has not only himself committed the crime of high treason in the most aggravated sense of the word, and in many respects and different ways; but has also been accessary to the same being committed by others; not to mention that his whole conduct and administration has been one continued succession of arbitrary, ambitious and self-interested proceedings, in open defiance of the Laws, Religion and good Morals (which he not only despised himself, but even endeavoured to abolish by public ordonnances) : it is OUR firm opinion that Count *John Frederick Struensee* is GUILTY of the said crimes, and that he deserves the punishment inflicted thereon in the Danish Code of Laws, Book VI. Chap. iv. Art. 1.

We

We therefore judging accordingly (and to set an example of horror and detestation for such crimes to others) declare it to be JUST and RIGHT, that he be punished according to the following

SENTENCE:

" Count *John Frederick Struensee* has for-
" feited his honour, his life and his estate;
" he shall be degraded from his dignity as
" Count, and all other dignities that have
" been conferred upon him; his coat of
" arms, which he had as Count, shall be
" broken by the executioner; his right
" hand, and afterwards his head, shall be
" cut off while alive; his body shall be
" quartered, and laid upon the wheel,
" but his head and hand shall be stuck
" upon a pole."

Given by the King's Commission at the Castle of Christiansburg, April 25, 1772.

J. K. Juel Wind.　　　G. A. Bræm.
(L. S.)　　　　　　　(L. S.)

H. Stampe 12 JY 62 Luxdorph.
(L. S.)　　　　　　　(L. S.)

A. G. Carstens.　　　Kofoed Ancher.
(L. S.)　　　　　　　(L. S.)

J. E. E. Schmidt.　　　F. C. Sevel.
(L. S.)　　　　　　　(L. S.)

Owe Guldberg.
(L. S.)

THE

THE

ROYAL APPROBATION

OF

THE SENTENCE

PRONOUNCED UPON

John Frederick Struenſee.

WE hereby approve, in every reſpect, of the Sentence pronounced by the Com-miſſion of Inquiſition, which we had appointed at our caſtle of Chriſtanſburg, upon *John Fre-derick Struenſee*, on account of his having, in more than one reſpect, committed the *Crimen læſæ Majeſtatis* in the higheſt degree; " That he has " forfeited his honour, his life, and his eſtates; " that he ſhall be degraded from his dignity as " Count, and all other dignities conferred upon him; " that his coat of arms, which he had as Count, " ſhall be broken by the executioner; that his

L 3   " right

" right hand, and afterwards his head fhall be cut
" off while alive ; and that his body fhall be quar-
" tered and laid upon the wheel, but his head and
" hand fhall be ftuck upon a pole." Whereupon thofe whom it concerns, are commanded to
act accordingly.

Given at our Caftle of Chriftianfburg, April 27,
  1772.

CHRISTIAN.

12 JY 62

O. THOTT.

LUXDORPH.   A. SCHUMACHER.
DONS.   HOYER.

THE END.

CPSIA information can be obtained
at www.ICGtesting.com
Printed in the USA
BVHW01s0328110418

513069BV00011B/106/P